Touching Smyrna

André Leferge

Printed and bound in India by
Authentic Media, Secunderabad 500 067, India
E-mail: printing@ombooks.org

DEDICATION

This book was inspired by courageous and principled men women and families engaged in the struggle for social justice around the world. It is my hope that their contributions to my life can be shared with you. In view of the injustice currently operating in many of their countries, their locations and surnames have been omitted.

Adnan and Neelam

Francois and Beatrice

Matt and Lori

Moise and Elizabeth

Peter and Cynthia

Sanna, Dashni and Debbie

Scott, Gayla, Jordan, Andy, Erin, Ladonna, Blair and Jon

Steven and Helen

Sukhen and Puspa

ACKNOWLEDGEMENTS

Originality is such an impossible quality to verify, and it is likely that many others should be acknowledged here. However significant influences must be attributed to the following people. Some are authors, others friends.

Barney Coombs

Berni Comissiong

Cyril Coombs

Dallas Willard

Ernie Addicott

Gary Lamb

Gill Morgan

Jeremy Russell

Lance Lambert

Mark and Fiona Stanton

Martin Robinson

Matt Summerfield

Nigel and Christine Lewis

Patrick Dixon

Paul Little

Paul Stockley

Pete Gilbert

Phil Hulks

Phil Kingham

Richard Foster

Rob Bell

Rob Hudson

Sam Moyo

Tom Macgregor

Tom Wright

Tony Campolo

Utsa Patnaik

Viv Grigg

CONTENTS

FOREWORD

It's not often that a book grabs your attention and makes you want to keep turning the pages. It's not common that you get caught up with, and find yourself caring about, the characters. Or that the pace is exhilarating. Or that the breadth and scope of the book is breathtaking.

And dare I say it — it's even rarer that such a book is, in its very essence, a book about living faith in Christ. Yet this book is all of those things. I read the first draft while on a car journey through the beautiful Highlands of Scotland, and didn't want to put it down. The resonances of Africa and of the USA felt real and immediate, the characters very human.

For this is not merely a book of fiction. I know the author well. I know of his passions and his experiences. And this book reflects them well, and does so creatively, yet accurately. None of these scenarios are wildly fanciful. Far from it. In many instances the details are as real as the backdrop is accurate. The tragedies and the triumphs, the transformations and the truculence are not only viable, but in many cases happened in much the way you read them here.

For above all else this is a book about God's heart for his world, and the potential of individuals, captivated by his freedom, to make a difference his way in his world. The book is a journey towards what authentic, lived-out discipleship might look and feel like: not just internally and ego-centrically, but on a world stage. Which, after all, was the missional drive behind the commission of Christ to the first disciples. To make disciples of all nations (*tè ethnè*); of every people group, everywhere.

The call to authentic discipleship is at one and the same time a call to personal integrity and intimacy with Christ, and a call to global engagement and transformation. None of it is possible without the empowering and infilling of the person and power

i

of God's life and breath, his Holy Spirit. This transcends circumstances; goes beyond what we practically have or do not have. This is what truly defines who and how we are, and can be in God's world. These are the riches of Christ; ours at his expense. This book provokes us to live radically for him and make the difference. I urge you to read it, enjoy it, be irritated by it. And to seek to live it.

Pete Gilbert.

(Founder, DNA discipleship course)

Years ago in the inner city a young girl came to our programme with lice in her hair. An elder at the church said this about me as I hugged the girl who was being made fun of by other children that had come from the suburbs with their grandfather, 'Gayla thinks you have to touch people in order to touch them.' André Leferge in 'Touching Smyrna' causes us to pause and think about what social justice really means in a shattered world. He reminds us that we need to physically touch those who are suffering in order to touch them with God's amazing love. As you read this book and as you reflect on its ministry lessons you will be compelled to respond.

Gayla Cooper Congdon.

(Founder, Amor Ministries)

PREFACE

'Why Smyrna?' would be a legitimate question to ask. Let me attempt to explain; first, why was this book written at all?

Having worked closely with those seeking to represent God in over 20 countries and across four continents, I have had the privilege of spending quality time with some truly incredible people. They have inspired this book; many of the scenarios found in its pages have played out in my life or theirs, though the story itself is entirely fictional and not one of its characters is real.

It has been part of my world to have guns poked at my face, to submit myself to uniformed banditry in customs sheds and to observe the poisonous fruits of injustice first hand as manifested in the lives of the poor. I have become increasingly disappointed by the behaviour of governments, often represented by shiny uniforms and officious, occasionally even smiling faces.

I'm sorry to admit that the illusions I once lived with about the appropriate use of power by worthy representatives have been exposed by the harsh realities of being on the receiving end of a callous disregard for intrinsic human worth, perception management and outright lies.

If the bible is true, and God is who the bible proclaims him to be, then authentic transformational leadership is needed in order to route our human race into civilization from a state of rebellion against his genuinely altruistic sovereignty. Where he lives nobody is poor, or suffers lack, or cries out for justice. We have chosen to live elsewhere but have been invited back.

Our human systems of rule have a common problem, a fundamental flaw. Whether they are the huge structures of nations, multinational companies, or organisations such as the UN or the European Community; or smaller outfits like UEFA, local authorities or families. The problem shared across all organisations run by men and women is poor character displayed in leadership.

We have had (and indeed still have) powerful leaders. I'm sure you can think of some; people who have seized power, or been handed it and used that power for good or ill, usually both.

In our own lives we have experienced the leadership of our father and or mother, except where there has been tragic loss, to our great cost. We know in detail what that leadership looked like, the exact nature of the group being led, and the degree of justice experienced, principally by us.

A personal fascination of mine is with the leadership found in the church. Don't misunderstand me, I don't mean any one named church with its Proper Noun title, no, I mean the worldwide church. Tony Campolo, a man I greatly admire, likens the church to an unfaithful woman; in fact I think his language may be a little stronger than that. However he urges us to grapple with a fact: 'She is your mother.' He calls us to love her, honour her.

In the church there is a wide range of levels of leadership to observe. People that lead committees, meetings, projects, missionary movements, congregations, denominations, dioceses, and a host of other responsibilities. Many of them do it terribly. I have personally contributed to some awful decisions as well as some good ones, often reflecting with some chagrin on what God must think of my performance. I am sure many other strugglers do the same.

Coming to the letter from God to the church at Smyrna found in the bible in the book of the Apocalypse, the 'drawing back of the curtain' — more commonly known as the book of Revelation: the letter was dictated to John, one of the twelve first apostles of Christ. It gives us a little but important glimpse of how God views authenticity.

What John writes down comes across as if the author is scarily aware of the exact circumstances and behaviour of the group; just as if he was circulating among them, one with them — which of course he was.

He writes that he knows about both their poverty and their suffering. There's one in the eye for those whose motive for relating to God is to avoid pain and get rich.

In Smyrna there was leadership which stood for something; it had attracted opposition. And something else, it had got some decisions very right. It appears that the church was engaged in some kind of titanic struggle, with more trouble to come.

The letter to Smyrna makes two declarations: one, that despite living with suffering and poverty the church was rich; the other, that those who opposed it claimed to be led by God but in fact were not.

This kind of invites us to apply two tests for authenticity which run as threads throughout the little story in this book: 'Does God call you rich?' and 'Does God call you "mine"?'

And so perhaps as you walk with me through the pages that follow you might want to ponder those two little questions: 'Does God call me rich?' Does God call me "mine"?'

André Leferge.

----

1.   IN THE WILDERNESS

Casper Alexander Scales, founder and owner of one of two companies short listed for Tech Startup of the Year honours, was pleased with himself.

Absent mindedly, he ran a finger down the nape of the sleeping Candice's neck gently stroking her ash blonde tousled hair. A flying cheerleader, physically lovely but possibly intellectually limited, Candice was a short term affair undertaken rather too lightly on his return from the excitement of the last weeks of his final semester. She had been flattered to be seen with an ex-Aztec, especially one with a top Masters from an Ivy League University, self-made and living on Point Loma.

Now that she had given herself to him completely, while happy to accept everything on offer he felt distinctly uncomfortable and dissatisfied that he could not reciprocate. She really wasn't that interesting and he was already feeling stifled. There was no doubt about it, she would have to go. Extracting himself from the relationship with minimum collateral damage would be an interesting new challenge, and one which might set the tone for the future if he could perfect a technique.

He quietly slipped from the bed, his bare feet padding as softly as possible across the apartment. His finger hovered over the ice button, but in view of the noise it would make, he reluctantly drew a glass of ice cold water from the refrigerator and stepped through the sliding door onto the balcony looking out across the Point Loma skyline.

It was early Sunday morning and in a not uncommon moment of self-indulgence, Casper reflected on what had been the most successful year of his life to date. It had culminated in a heady final month during which he had ticked off every remaining item on his personal college bucket list (a wish list of 20 things to do before his college life came to an end) including taking home the homecoming queen, contributing to the Dartmouth Review, and graduating in the top 10 of MBA students at Tuck.

Unquestionably, the triumphant sequence was capped by his choosing the night before Dartmouth College Commencement Day to successfully complete the Blue Light Challenge; an extreme form of Dartmouth's tradition of streaking in which the participant attempts to evade campus security personnel and activate all 31 emergency buttons on the code blue phones while buck naked. Having achieved from this the requisite notoriety his peers would expect from an outgoing top receiver in the college's Big Green Football Team, he could leave with head held high, able through mere eye contact to attain the level of mutual understanding and communication that only fellow streakers can share.

Despite the deep satisfaction his driven nature derived from these achievements, he was most pleased with himself for what had initially been a distraction, and had not even featured on the bucket list.

Casper lit a thin cigar and reflected on the day Droneview Reality Inc. had begun: on The Green at Dartmouth with Marcus and

Chip, his campus best friends. Marcus Postlethwaite was a geek with almost no athletic ability. He shaved infrequently, washed sporadically, developed most impressive acne and had that irrepressible *joie de vivre* peculiar only to madcap inventors with restless minds. Marcus was at Dartmouth courtesy of a full scholarship to Thayer on account of strings pulled by his Guidance Counselor and Principal at High School. He was an unmistakable engineering genius and worthy of the favours granted. He was also the best 'Call of Duty' player on campus, a digital legend — and in Casper's opinion the finest online team ally available.

Chip (Charles Broderick Goldstein the 3rd, to his family) was a nut whose principal qualities were goofing around, kicking a football and playing guitar. His dad owned huge amounts of real estate across California and having gained dual Mexican citizenship through his second marriage (Alejandra was only eight years older than Chip) had got into the Yucatan before most people realized what it would become. Thousands of his acres of dirt cheap jungle had undergone modest development, then municipalization, then massive investment, and finally achieved real estate prices higher than anyone could have hoped.

Chip was torn between two dreams: getting drafted to the NFL as a kicker; or launching a band and making it big down in Nashville. Neither could happen — he lacked the commitment to deliver on either of them, preferring socializing and online gaming to practicing, settling for outstanding but not stratospheric talent. He had daddy's money behind him but carried his rich kid privileges with an easy grace which made him totally cool. He could pick his friends, and had unsurprisingly chosen Casper.

Marcus, inspired by watching drones in the Swat Valley on CNN had been messing around with remote control helicopters, a laptop and some bits of plastic. He'd come up with a really neat manoeuvrable home made drone which he could fly using his laptop and a gaming joystick. Anxious to see what his Heath Robinson military–grade robot helicopter could do one Saturday evening in May, Marcus had hurried down to The Green, full of adrenaline and awed excitement muttering profanities in expectation of what his creation could achieve.

The Green, the oldest and most familiar area of Dartmouth's historic site, was the obvious place for students to hang out on a warm balmy evening. With plenty of space on the neatly manicured lawns and only a few trees to worry about, it seemed the most logical place on Earth in which to test an unmanned aircraft.

There he found Chip and Casper, sitting under a tree jamming with their guitars outside the library. They were of course instantly recruited for inclusion in flight testing, and guitars abandoned, they excitedly joined the ground crew. There was of course no sense of responsibility nor any tendency towards risk management found among the three. The maiden voyage of 'Marcusdrone 1' lasted just 15 seconds.

Sitting watching the lights of the boats in the bay Casper smiled in recollection of those epic 15 seconds. In hindsight, the launch site was perilously close to the historic buildings, and it was not unpredictable that the machine would fly straight up in the air, lose a tail rotor, begin to spin wildly, go into random attack mode and take out a ground floor window of the Baker Memorial Library, scattering students and staff in its path and showering patrons of the library with glass.

In a country renowned for litigation it was perhaps surprising that no suits were filed and the college took the generosity of Chip's dad into account when assessing the need for imposing sanctions. Things could have been worse.

Within four weeks of that maiden voyage, 'Marcusdrone 4' was capable of making reliable flights, and soon after that 'Marcusdrone 6' was equipped with a camera and making nocturnal visits to various windows in the Freshmen student dorms facilitating some highly regrettable YouTube and Instagram postings.

It was these photo shoots which got Casper thinking about commercial photographic uses.

Just for something to do, during a weekend break in Cancun 'Marcusdrone 7' was employed by the three friends to shoot and upload a video of the condo in which they stayed which, along with the whole block was offered for rent by Chip's dad. The results were spectacular. Uploaded to YouTube the video, including some sequences of the drone itself and the guys launching it, went viral. Marcus' ability to manipulate Google's search ranking for the site made online bookings of the condo and the remainder of the block take off as readily as the drone had.

After coaching the local office manager for a few hours, Marcus persuaded him to part with a significant sum for his flying pet robot. The transaction paid for the weekend and an upgrade to 'Marcusdrone 8' back in Dartmouth. Commercial possibilities began to dawn in Casper's agile mind.

Marcus, meanwhile, got together with a couple of his geeky mates and came up with a neat template for inserting video into online info packs and property outlines and Chip's presentation skills made the training videos for using drones very simple to follow and easy on the eye for male and female realtors alike.

As part of his MBA course Casper spent some time in Dubai where a placement at the Dragon Mart put him in relationship with Chinese manufacturing. The Chinese, offering incredibly low production costs and high technical skills enabled Casper to bring low priced state–of–the–art camera technology and high performance, easy–to–fly drones designed by Marcus to the US realty market.

The synergy of skills and contacts of the three friends began to manifest itself. Chip's natural charm and easy manner made him an amazingly persuasive salesman. Casper's 'make it happen' leadership, problem solving and eye for risk and opportunity made him a natural strategic leader. Marcus couldn't help improving on design, and loved working with the Chinese.

Calls were placed to students' parents who held strategic commercial positions, recommendations were made in the right places, Twitter trended, everyone wanted the product, sales went ballistic. Prices were high and costs low, so the margins were incredible. Order processing, packing and shipping was sub-contracted to a logistics specialist, technical support to a subsidiary of the Chinese manufacturer and everything went nuts. This was especially so when Fry's came in with a deal for development and then buy-out if successful, of a version of the drones for private personal use.

At 26 years old, three months into full time employment, 16 months after the first product was shipped Casper was positioned as the largest provider of what was now seen as essential equipment by the majority of top players in realty; to show prospective clients literally all over their property portfolios. He had a huge order in for a personal version 'Skycam' which would go to market with a massive pay per click marketing plan via Facebook and online news platforms next month.

The three friends had carried little of the weight of day-to-day manufacture, production or delivery and yet had found themselves commercially successful beyond their dreams.

Although he hadn't broached the subject with the others yet, Casper was ready to sell an exciting new (probably award-winning) company to the highest bidder before the end of the year. He was up for for another challenge and had inventors and entrepreneurs bombarding him with fascinating projects every day.

He came in from the balcony and glanced at Candice. She was still sleeping so he decided to let her lie in for a while. He told himself that this was to indulge her, but the reality was that he could use the time alone at his laptop without disturbance. He had two rather secretive interests to service.

Way back in eighth grade he had been introduced to pornography. Back then he'd got hold of some magazines with his high school friends and they'd giggled and guffawed with titillated over-excitement as their hormones turned confused cartwheels and their amoral brains over-rode any prudish advice parents and Sunday school teachers had given them.

It was still cool and acceptable to look at porn all the way through high school. Nudges, winks and leery expressions alluded to the subject almost daily. When the internet invaded all of their lives, he and his friends continually exchanged web addresses and methods of circumventing school and parental controls by the use of proxy servers.

For the others, indulgence in soft porn seemed the most natural approach to the opportunities presented by a digital age with decreasing censorship. It was all good harmless fun, nobody got hurt and adolescent life was a digital bowl of cherries. Pixels titillated, and real women with flesh and emotions and a range of qualities beyond the visual could wait for a while. Self-gratification was a click and a private space away.

For Casper it was not all heady excitement and fun. Very early on in his exposure to porn his fascination turned to obsession. He found himself thinking of naked women and lewd acts every hour of the day. The amount of pleasure derived by the naughtiness of checking out magazines quickly diminished, and he found that obtaining the mental excitement and arousal he'd first enjoyed with centrefolds and written articles required video, then more diverse and bizarre images and scenes on into hard core material even he would objectively describe as sick. These days, aware that his interest placed him in the 'out of the ordinary' category of voyeurs he was careful only to indulge himself in online stimulation when nobody was around. He always set his browser to incognito mode so as long as he didn't use a system where an administrator had access to controls beyond his reach, his browsing history was untraceable.

With Candice on the scene, opportunities were more limited. However there was something about the possibility of discovery that added an edge of excitement to his secretive self-pleasuring world. This morning as he watched the screen, absorbed in the writhing, moaning ecstatic scenes before his eyes, part of his attention was reserved for watching for movement from Candice.

Finally, breaking free from his reverie, he turned and tapped in the address of another frequently visited website: CityTradeIndex dot Biz.

CityTradeIndex was his favourite offshore spread betting and CFD (cost for difference) account provider. Based in Bulgaria the site facilitated two forms of tax-free high stakes and high risk commodities trading. Spread betting was simple enough: he would pick a commodity that he was sure would rise or fall in value, and bet an amount per incremental gain or loss. For example, a particularly lucrative coup had arisen from his quick reaction to the Icelandic ash cloud incident in April 2011 which led to a significant fall in the price of airline fuel when demand for it dropped by over 40 million barrels during the crisis period. He had picked up $10 000 US on the drop, and bet the whole amount on an immediate pick up as soon as British Airways flew a test flight in May and produced data effectively minimizing disruption from that time on. Prices rose above the previous norm, and what had caused financial and commercial nightmares for most of the world produced sweet dreams for him.

His choices of San Diego State University for his bachelors course (an invitation from the Aztecs and a Point Loma home address owing to his dad being in the US Navy had made that a no-brainer) and then a shoo-in to Tuck enabled two related fields to develop: first, an in depth understanding of the commodities markets from some of the finest economics teachers in the world; second, some close relationships with several friends whose parents had sent them to top colleges in preparation for inheriting significant family investment businesses.

Why spread betting worked so well for Casper was that the company set its price according to how the commodity was trading at the moment of placing the bet. If Casper had accurate information affecting future price, he had a sure–fire winner. His sources were excellent and his nerve and speed of reaction well suited to the volatility of that approach to the markets.

He had intended to fund his passage through college by betting his generous allowance on commodities. However, making the football team had completely covered his college fees, releasing all of his substantial trading profits to less mundane activities, including cars, holidays and the startup funding for Droneview Realty Inc.

One particular conversation with the semi inebriated and star–struck father of a SDSU friend called Joe Leihmann had opened up a whole world of easy profit making to Casper. Joe's dad (clearly trying to impress him) had done something the professors in class had emphasized over and over. Never disclose live information while the market is running.

Old man Leihmann was into Africa in a big way. He had worked out that in Francophone West Africa in particular there were some great opportunities for big agrochemical companies to acquire and develop huge tracts of land.

The method was simple and easy to achieve: first, displace the indigenous, inefficient subsistence farmers and their motley array of family buildings; then, insert modern agricultural methods with external irrigation and mechanization investments; finally, convert what was previously economically unproductive land into huge mechanized farming conglomerates as seen in the US Midwest. This in turn gave rise to high quality export businesses to lucrative Middle Eastern and European markets, raising the GDP of the subject nation, and of course the balance sheet of the multinational corporation behind the development.

In Mali, Burkina Faso and Southern Sudan in particular, easily persuaded officials made obtaining land rights a relatively inexpensive formality, and cash cropping on a grand scale quickly followed on. The humanitarian impact was minimal — the indigenous farmers were hardly worse off chasing a living in the cities than they had been on their little patches of dirt and where there had been previously inefficient subsistence farming there was now world class agricultural production providing much needed food to the hungry markets of Asia and Europe.

Unlike the complicated lobbying scene, agrochemical companies were forced to navigate in Europe, the under-developed legal systems in sub–Saharan Africa meant that the use of emerging genetically modified strains of seed could go unchallenged by any potentially contaminated neighbours. In the unlikely event of harmful effects occurring they would be experienced by people with no voice or legal standing. Everyone was a winner, but few individually gained more than Casper.

The agrochemical companies were the place to position his investments, with sure–fire returns for years to come. Further side lines also formed. With the increase in cash cropping, the production of local staples came under pressure and the price of maize in particular rose in unprecedented fashion so investment in efficient maize producing companies local to the pressure points also saw great returns. There would also be spread betting possibilities around the price of food falling in Europe and Asia, and continuing to rise in sub–Saharan Africa in the future.

Casper had decided to experiment with these opportunities. After all, the US markets were so completely riddled with insider trading that there were very few genuine steals available there. With regulation tightening and all sorts of horror stories about squealers dropping their mates' details to the IRS and FBI to save their own skins when Lehmann Bros and Enron went bang, even acting on information from trusted friends was not tempting enough for someone as smart as him.

June that year had brought him a wonderful result and having cashed in his long positions he had made what had so far emerged as his finest play in the investment game so far. He spread bet everything on the maize price rising sharply the following year, and he was right.

This morning he spent some minutes planning where next to go long. He decided that further price hikes were likely in Burkina Faso and Mali. Reuters was reporting that there was some kind of Al Qaeda trouble in Northern Mali so refugees were flooding across the border; food was bound to be scarce. He positioned his predictions accordingly.

He calculated that if he was even close to being right he could buy a top specification 35 foot sport fishing boat and a Ram 1500 pickup truck to tow it, next July. From past performance July was looking increasingly likely to be the best month to cash in. He would keep checking those numbers but once he placed his bets he was locked in.

He loved the privacy and secrecy of the futures and spread betting world. It was this that brought him fully alive. It set his pulse racing, and he would find himself checking throughout the day, every day, how the figures were shaping up. It was all about the numbers and nothing, not the excitement of making a long in–zone catch in front of a sellout crowd; not sex, nor not even his lurid, porn fuelled fantasy world could affect him like this.

Having indulged himself enough he decided it was probably time to get the day started, so he fired up the Keurig, fixed two skinny lattes and woke up the now stirring Candice.

Their breakfast was taken at his favourite waterfront café. Sunday was indulgence day and he selected the house speciality, a Mexican omelette of outrageous proportions. Candice had the fruit salad with fat free yoghurt but looked hungrily at Casper's groaning plate. She had been hungry for six years now, one price of flying cheerleader fame. Being a flying cheerleader meant being chucked up in the air like a toy doll, turning gymnastic somersaults and spins at impossible heights. It looked spectacular from the stands, and for every girl like her, there were thousands of hopeful replacements busily starving and practicing in readiness for the opportunity to don a miniskirt and lycra.

The pressure was incredible and she knew that the clock was ticking on the demands she was making of her body. It would not be long now before the team got itself a replacement blonde gymnast, and the glory she now had would become old photographs and empty costumes in her mom's apartment.

After breakfast it was time for church. They had a little routine going. He took the Lexus convertible, she her Jeep Wrangler daddy had bought her for college. It wouldn't look good if they arrived together from breakfast — cohabitation was not really compatible with holding ministry positions.

Ablaze was a fairly young church plant into an affluent suburb down towards Mission Bay, so there were plenty of volunteering opportunities. He led the worship, and she being new, was waiting to be asked to sing at one of the mics. She had the face for it.

This morning's set was particularly good. Casper was on form and held just the right tone of brokenness in his voice as he led the congregation in a rendition of Hillsong's 'Hosannah.'

> *'Break my heart for what breaks yours, everything I have for your Kingdom's cause,'* he sang.

Absolutely no sense of irony occurred to his transcendent mind. He was carried on a wave of euphoria conjured by a combination of music exactly to his taste and inspirational out of body concepts that spoke to his soul of goodness and peace. It never really occurred to him to ask himself if God liked the song. Why should it? This was church after all, and singing music to the congregation's taste was a vital part of the culture. Casper was excellent at it, a superb worship leader, very good looking, with deep rich tones to his Negro voice. Muscular, prosperous, skilled and charismatic; he was the perfect choice for an onstage role.

Garry, the preacher, was fresh out of seminary leading his first plant. He was a bright kid, smart, handsome and personable, with a great history bachelor's degree followed by a Masters at Princeton. Following what he described as a profound and decisive encounter with God at a Young Life camp in his mid–teens he'd done some volunteering on a house building project down in Juarez in his first year at college. That had changed the course of his life, angled his direction of travel towards Princeton. Ministry was his focus for the foreseeable future.

After Juarez he'd done a lot of volunteering down at the projects and had a great understanding of mission. If he was honest he saw himself primarily as an up–and–coming pioneering leader with a bit more edge than some of the big shots who'd already made it. He was now building Ablaze into a smart church that could finance a shed load of altruistic effort in the years ahead and was careful to pack his ministry team with social elites. He'd learned that people with money liked to be able to control its use when thinking about donating, so he structured the various committees around those who contributed the most financially.

There were any number of books and courses on how to build a successful church available to an aspiring leader, and Garry had read them all.

A charismatic platform team soon builds a smart crowd of onlookers, and it was his ministry team's job to work that crowd. Everyone had targets to achieve, numbers to hit, and standards to strive for. This was a great team and he had every intention of building a mega–church.

It was a lonely role though, and if he was honest, joyless. He'd long ago lost any sense of the kind of personal interaction with God that had led to his life direction decision making; opting these days to know *about* God rather than relate to him, if he really was out there. The concept of God had for him somehow morphed into the construct of Christendom and that into machine of church. He was persuaded of the facts about God. He could explain very eloquently what they were but in truth he was constrained by the constituency he had built to finance the programmes he ran; to preach what itching ears wanted to hear.

This morning Garry's treatise ran over the recent support Obama had given gay marriage, and the mass unemployment and repos affecting church members all over the US. Much of this could be tracked back to Washington where the administration had failed to tackle the economic crisis, and the greed behind toxic loan granting. Instead huge amounts of time and legislation had been devoted to distracting healthcare issues. The country was a mess, and what was bad for the US was bad for God. How else would the advance of the right to life, liberty and the pursuit happiness across the world continue if the mother lode sickened? How could God bless America if His standards were not espoused by his greatest ally on Earth? Until Washington grew a God fearing conscience and resumed a biblical approach to administration, what stood between the country and judgment?

The church prayed, as it often did, for change in Washington leading to an upturn in San Diego, particularly of course among the needy there financed by the thriving of the congregation and others like them.

There was some presentation by Buzz the youth coordinator about a house building mission trip across the border to Tijuana. Garry had kept up the links for over a decade with the mission organization concerned. He had been thinking though for some time now that what he had become wasn't really compatible with the idealistic approach of the missionary folks who'd got him into ministry.

It made him distinctly uncomfortable to think about their way of operating: on a knife edge, honouring unprofessional flea bitten Mexican pastors and favouring the long term interests of the weak throughout the process rather than the system that served them. He had learned better from smarter outfits, and was toying with the idea of making a challenge to them in the near future.

Casper wasn't listening to the presentation. He was checking commodity prices on his iPhone. Candice was; she had been asked to help out with some of the girls and was very concerned about the conditions she may have to face next April.

After the service Casper and Candice sipped iced lattes in the newly refurbished church café, exchanging small talk with a glittering selection of influential congregants. They slipped away as early as possible for a shellfish lunch at the Blue Wave, and back to Casper's dad's apartment for their regular Sunday afternoon return to the bedroom.

Casper decided that he had a good thing going here and ending the relationship may not be in his amusement interests and throughout their loving did his best to focus on Candice; trying desperately to stop his mind and imagination straying to the more exotic images he had been engorging alone.

2. HOME

'Where is that stupid girl? I will beat her until her ass bleeds when I find her.'

Eve's little body stiffened involuntarily at the sound of her name and her face contorted with fear as her father's booming voice carried across the dusty, rubbish strewn street. She knew he was as mean as a startled mamba, and would not hesitate to harm her if the mood took him. She immediately abandoned her carefree conversation with Fatoumata and Bibata, lifelong friends in the large village of Djigouera and hurried to the little compound that was home.

It was June in Burkina Faso and the burning sun had mercilessly scorched all but the toughest scrub into brittle arid submission. Her bare feet, toughened by years of running on the scorching shard–strewn red–brown earth carried her urgently and weightlessly back across the street.

Ibrahim was feeling especially irritable this morning. A vicious cocktail of ills had conspired to ruin his mood. Firstly, he had been drinking dolo (the local millet beer) last night and his aching head contained a brain that was sluggish; secondly Burkina Faso had been defeated in a crunch African Cup of Nations match, to a wonder goal from Nigeria; thirdly the price of food was rising and he was worried about the family's stocks lasting until the next harvest; fourthly his first wife Mariam was sick and this had an impact on his Sunday morning routine.

His second wife Dina was of no use. She was heavily pregnant, and he was still quite taken with his third wife Bintou's looks so tended not to be too brutal towards her. Consequently she was lazier than Mariam and Dina and although they hated her he would see to it that they didn't harm her.

In order to get some tea and millet porridge he was apt to yell at Mariam's children, and especially her eldest girl, Eve.

Eve had a quality about her that made her both irritating and interesting. She had an unbreakable spirit. He had beaten her severely many times and often spoke harshly to her. She never answered him back, obviously, as the consequences would have been terrible for her; but there was something in her eyes that told him she feared though did not respect him. She was damn good at domestic chores however and his first choice for picking on when Mariam was too ill to work, something becoming increasingly regular.

Catching sight of Eve scampering across the compound towards him he cursed her for not being immediately available when he'd looked for her.

'Idiot girl, always wasting time up and down the street where is my tea kettle? Bring me some food!'

'I will fetch your kettle father and I will hurry to prepare food.' Eve was careful not to meet his eye. She had received many hard punches for what he described as a bold look, something he would not tolerate. She couldn't turn it off, so she turned it away.

Ibrahim's friend Idrissa would be along shortly and there was much to lament about last night's game. Time was short and he was keen to have things ready for an important morning of post mortem punditry. It would be a helpful distraction from food, a subject that was filling him with fear and must surely soon be addressed.

Eve quickly fetched a few sticks of firewood and the dry reed grass for kindling. She lit the fire with one tiny match, filled the kettle from the family's clay water pot which she had earlier filled at the village's new pump. Placing the kettle carefully on the untidy arrangement of medium sized stones around which the lit wood burned, she stood back, hands on hips, head on one side checking that it was heating properly. After a short time she was able to mix a little millet porridge with the boiling water, adding in some sauce made with leaves of the baobab tree just along the street. The family was very poor, and Eve would not eat today. Only Ibrahim would have breakfast, and that was because he was expecting company.

Eve did not hate her father. She had been taught at church that forgiveness was the key to her own escape from the misery of being a victim. Every night she prayed for him, hoping that he would be happier the next day. So far her prayers had not been answered. She knew that to repay evil with good was an offering very pleasing to the God they spoke about at church. From the description the pastor gave, Eve wanted very much to know this amazing provider as a loving compassionate father. Her young mind was full of questions. Since she'd started praying God hadn't provided very much, and there was very little evidence of him coming through on the compassion either.

She day-dreamed about God now as she often had, but he seemed very far from her as she skillfully blew on her fire and coaxed it into perfect suitability for brewing tea; then withdrew respectfully from the cooking area. Her father, Ibrahim would take things from here. Brewing tea was an art, and since he did little else, or so it seemed to Eve, he would be the family's foremost artist.

With his porridge steaming in a little wooden bowl Ibrahim came and hunched down on a little three legged stool, one of very few pieces of furniture the family owned, and began the long process of brewing Touareg tea. He would be absorbed in this activity for much of the morning, serving himself and Idrissa from small battered shot glasses acquired way back in his father's day.

He reflected on life as he stared into the flames. None of his children went to school and he really struggled to remember all of their names, nor exactly how many there were. If asked he would need to call his wives together and they would tell him. The women and oldest boys carried out all of the work associated with daily life, including working the fields. Ibrahim had long since ceased to make any contribution, preferring to drive the necessary activity with his harsh words and quick fist.

The modest patch of land he had received from the local chief, a distant uncle when he first married, was his kingdom. Here in his compound he reigned supreme and untouchable in his nuclear family, accountable to no–one. Demands could be made of him of course but his decisions and his word here were final.

He sat on his stool repeatedly pouring and re–pouring the foaming tea, looking for the perfect strength. Ibrahim's mind drifted back to the meeting in which he and his father had formally met the chief, Uncle Lamin, immediately prior to the wedding with Mariam. The meeting had been to discuss whether he might be granted some land on which to raise a family. Lamin was so called because he was born on a Friday, as every good Moslem knows. He smiled wryly. Good Moslem; that was hardly a description of any of the family! At that time the excitement of a forthcoming family wedding had given him some passing prominence and good will. Land allocation was very much tied up with ancestral lineage and worship. Effectively, Uncle Lamin owned all the land around their village and his word on allocation was unchallengeable. A good word that day held a lifetime of implications.

Despite his own family's attendance at the local Catholic Church, Ibrahim's father had been careful to make sure his relationship with Uncle Lamin, both an Imam and the family's main authority on contacting the spirits, was not compromised. There was freedom of religion in Burkina Faso, but not necessarily universal approval within families regarding religious choices.

Things had become complicated in his father's generation because at that time the Catholics had been the main source of effective anti malarial medicines. There had been some kind of a tie–up with the French authorities — anyway, they had dispensed the best drug. They had also been very insistent that attendance at Mass was a condition of medication. It was obvious that the medicine was effective as the survival rates of Catholic children were far better than non–Catholics. According to Ibrahim's father either their God or their medicine worked wonders. Whichever, having sons to work his fields was his priority, and being a pragmatic man, if that meant dragging the family to church, he'd considered it worth it.

In more recent years the government in partnership with the UN had started providing anti malarial treatments (though many said they often sent placebos just to win votes and certainly the results suggested that may be the case some years) the draw of the church had consequently become less powerful.

Over the years, Ibrahim's father had also many times sent a chicken or some grain to Uncle Lamin to contribute to the sacrifices needed to gain cooperation from the family spirits and appease the malevolent spirits at major traditional festivals and celebrations. There was warmth towards him and Ibrahim in the chief's compound and he had been obviously very much looking forward to their coming. Keeping their eyes below the level the chief's as they approached the old man, an indication of their subservience and groveling observance of the Mossi tribal mores, they had offered their opening pleasantries and had been served millet beer, and tô sauce in the saghbo; positive signs.

In true Mossi cultural fashion they had answered quickly and readily Uncle's enquiries about family members and how things were going within their compound and on their land. They had been pleased to assert that all was well with the women and children and that the animals were healthy, the crops well watered and growing.

The chief had smiled warmly and they listened patiently as he used the opportunity to remind them of the story of the village and the tribe, the importance of the ancestral spirits, of course his own place in the dynasty and how it all linked into worship of the supreme God, Allah — mainly through offerings to local spirits who could pass their devotion on up the chain.

The wily old fox had even suggested that seeing as Ibrahim was so close in lineage to him, he may one day lead the family thus it was important that he arrange for his own fetish when he built his compound if he was granted land. Ibrahim grimaced as he recalled conversations with his peers in later years, particularly immediately after the old man had died; which revealed he'd given them all the same line. Ibrahim caught himself, looking troubled for a moment. It was not wise to think unkindly of the dead. The spirits were constantly vigilant regarding dishonouring behaviour and could be quick to exact punishment.

Once granted land, he had been able to construct a mud brick house for himself and his new wife and things had gone well. Despite his wife's membership of the local Pentecostal church, something her mother had insisted on at the time of his proposal, Ibrahim had resisted any involvement there.

His occasional visits to Mass became more infrequent and with a change in local priests he dropped out of attendance altogether. He built a little fetish in the compound as directed by Uncle Lamin and he was always careful to appease the spirits by presenting whatever the local shaman suggested whenever something went seriously wrong or if he needed luck or guidance for any reason. When one of the children broke his leg, Ibrahim had taken a chicken and broken its leg over the fetish, binding it as the child's to speed recovery.

No man is an island, especially among the Mossi people and conversations with his Islamic friends helped him to understand the legitimacy of taking as many wives as possible and producing with them a large brood of children to work his land and keep him in his old age. This particular doctrine was in keeping with his animist roots; in fact the blend of spirituality in the area was a rich smörgåsbord of mainly misogynist and generational domineering, which brought stability and order to their peasant lives. Attendance at the mosque or at church was helpful to social standing in the community, as indeed was participation in the more tribal spiritual rituals. Ibrahim liked to keep everyone on side and was much liked by others in the community.

It had been many years since a tribal dispute had erupted in bloodshed. Even the practice of cutting the children's faces as infants to display for life the scars which identified their tribe had mainly fallen into disuse. Once a necessity, vital for survival and trading purposes, it had been outlawed by the government and very few practiced it. Ibrahim's lines of scars on cheeks and forehead were a sign as much of his age as his tribe.

The evidence of change was everywhere. Out here, far from the cities, technology had until recently been alien and incomprehensible. These days the sound of scooter van engines and taxis occasionally cut through the constant background chatter of crickets, birdsong and arguing lizards and frogs. The biggest and potentially most catastrophic recent change had been what had happened to the trade in cereals, the staple diet of the family. Last year traders had come and spoken with Ibrahim and his friends, promising good prices in CFA (African Francs) for some of the sacks of grain in their grain houses.

Every compound had at least one grain house, hand built, in the shape of a large earthenware pot thatched with reeds from the riverbank. Into this storehouse went the precious store of millet and rice that was the family's staple diet. Apart from these two cereals and a few chili and okra plants only the fruit from their one mango and two papaya trees provided the family with food throughout the year. They had a few goats and chickens, but these were rarely eaten, mainly at festivals. They also had a few cows watched over on their behalf by the expert Fulani drovers, and used to work the fields from time to time.

Ibrahim was very familiar with the concept of selling sacks of his millet in order to buy rice. Each year he would sell a proportion of his millet harvest, storing 20kg bags of rice alongside the millet. Their land had always been able to produce sufficient grain to allow for one meal of saghbo and rice per day for each family member. This millet based porridge would be flavoured with okra or chili, sometimes sour goat milk, and filled their stomachs adequately. Only Ibrahim took breakfast.

Since the new traders had come, things had got much more complicated. First they had offered him far more money for millet than was normally paid, soon after the harvest. Their offer was based on what they said was a strong export market to Mali, where people were prepared to pay far more for grain than those in Burkina Faso. This was a welcome move and it had led him to sell as much millet as possible to them.

Holding cash was difficult for Ibrahim. There were immediately so many demands on it, especially now. It was impossible to hide the fact that he was holding money. Part of the culture was to be instantly aware of who was doing well, and to gravitate towards them, making needs very clear. This was a problem because if needs were not met, especially within the family, the ancestral spirits could be commanded to visit mischief upon a person by collusion with the shaman, for a share in the returns. The results could be horrible for the victim of spiritual attack: disease or mental illness, bad luck — all kinds of misfortune could befall the one unwilling to meet the wider family's needs. It was far better to pay off the family members than take your chances.

To add to the squeeze brought about by this influx of demands, Ibrahim had a couple of personal appetites that the presence of cash did nothing to allay. He loved to sit out on the street with other heads of local families and drink dolo. While this was relatively inexpensive, it tended to happen more when he had more money in his pocket.

He was also aware that the sexual services of the servant children of a number of his friends were available for purchase. Even the thought of recalling these indulgent usually part drunken encounters caused a pleasing warm stirring sensation as blood flowed to his groin. With cash available he had simply been unable to restrain himself, though he had come to regret the financial impact in the weeks that followed.

It was in May that the region began to feel the impact of the traders' activities. Somebody had been stockpiling both millet and rice. The very small quantities available to buy were 1000 CFA above the normal acceptable price. This was not a major concern as everyone could just buy slightly less, tighten their belts and wait for the prices to fall again.

However, news that a child had died of starvation in a neighbouring village sent panic through the families. The severity of the shortage was beginning to bite and those weakened by malaria, yellow fever, malnutrition or infections from wounds or ulcers were very much at risk when food was short. Soon more deaths were reported among the very poor. Elderly people with few or no family to support them were reliant on the kindness of the villagers around them. When there was no surplus, there was nothing for them. Most children in the poorest families were eating only twice per week now.

The price of rice and millet doubled within three weeks. This was what the traders had been hoping for. This was why they had bought up supplies for good prices soon after harvest. They were now able to manufacture famine in both Mali and Burkina Faso. There was a real killing to be made. Ibrahim, along with many others used most of his remaining money to make sure he could at least have some food, while he could still afford it. The speed of price rises indicated that costs would continue to go up. This had happened before during famines produced by drought — though the cause of this particular crisis was manufactured, the outcome of a crude but brutally effective commercial strategy.

As a consequence of all this, Ibrahim knew for certain that sometime in the next few weeks the family's food would completely run out. He and the other family heads knew what to expect because of what had happened before in years when the rains had failed. Life would become a waiting game, waiting for the harvest to come before starvation picked them off one by one. He would focus on the matter after he'd enjoyed his tea with Idrissa.

In fact things were coming to financial crisis point a little faster than Ibrahim had thought. For now, as Idrissa came smiling into the compound, and Eve slipped away to comb her hair and make ready for church, football was the focus.

3.   SOMETHING NEW

Eve was 14 years old — but very small on account of her diet which lacked vitamins and protein. Nobody in the family had any education, and subjects like nutrition had no meaning for them. Of course there were NGOs which had aims and resources that could help educate and provide for her. However the reality for families like Eve's was that the scale of the need in the country was beyond available supply. They were too inaccessible to be easily reached and nobody really wanted the hassle of moving supplies too far from the source. There was plenty of need for the NGOs to meet, providing the necessary evidence of activity, closer to hand.

She drifted into the mud brick hut. The bricks had been hand cut by her older brothers under supervision from Ibrahim, only two years ago. The effect of the rains had been to cause them to melt into rounded caricatures of their original shape. The house should last two more years before it needed renewing, depending on whether or not the rains caused flooding, in which case there was a chance it could collapse entirely much earlier. There were no windows, just steel shutters that allowed the hot winds to blow through, and a steel door, again shuttered to allow the passage of air. The roof was of corrugated iron, weighted down with mud blocks and supported by ageing timbers. The timbers themselves were protected from termites by the hens pecking around the house. Termites feared chickens and would seek safer places to forage for wood.

The sun beating down caused heat to radiate from the metal roof, raising the temperature inside to almost 52 degrees Celsius. During the daytime, the best place to keep cool was under the shade of the mango tree. Eve's mother Mariam lay over there every day now, on a home made short–legged litter, constructed of inexpensive woven reed on a simple wooden frame. She mentally had lost her way earlier in the year, and her confused mind rambled. Her memory and faculties profoundly failing, to the degree that Eve and her sisters had for a while regularly toileted her day and night to avoid the appalling mess she had begun to make. Her appetite long gone, she picked at what little food she could be offered, eating almost nothing. She was skin and bone, not long for this world.

Eve made her way past her own sleeping place inside the house, a tiny space on the floor, to the table in the corner, the only decent piece of furniture the family owned. Here she picked up her mother's comb and began to tease her hair into shape. One day she would be able to buy a fine wig, and look amazing like the more prosperous women in the smart dresses and matching hats, who sang in the choir. For now she had nothing, except the one dress she wore, which she would wash each night and hang up ready for the morning. One dress, her only possession, and she had been eight years old before she had worn clothing at all.

She had been looking forward to today, as had the entire congregation. Today was the day when Louis Oudraogo would visit the little church. Old man Oudraogo was a legend in the region, a mighty man of God some said. He was grandfather to the Pentecostal Church's Regional Supervisor, the first chief in his part of the country to accept the American missionary into his home in 1928, and the first to burn his own fetish.

The story went that back then, Louis Oudraogo — who at 25 was the recently appointed village chief at Yarbo near the Koloko Department over by the French Sudanese border — had listened to the American man, named Walter Lee, over tea in his compound for hours. Louis, an accomplished tea maker, had plied his skills with enthusiasm, and Walter, a black man whose first language was English patiently explained in heavily accented French the long journey of faith and shoe leather which had led him from California to Europe, on to what would become Senegal then to Ouagadougou and finally beyond the capital to here, the border between French Sudan and Upper Volta. The countries would not gain independence from France for a further 30 years. He claimed that his church born in the original Azusa Street revival meetings a decade earlier had called a time of prayer and fasting and there had received a message from the one Creator God that they were to carry his friendship to the Mossi people. Walter had described the form of the message as a *'parole de connaissance'* — 'a word of knowledge.'

Lee and his friends took the matter very seriously and researched the matter, discovering that the Mossi people were from West Africa. Funded by friends, they had been 'sent out' from their little church and travelled to Senegal via Europe. There they had been directed inland to Niger, and from there redirected to Upper Volta where they had indeed found the people to whom they believed God had sent them. To their dismay they found there was no common language, and spent a frustrated year learning French, which was widely spoken among the Mossi, and more accessible to Californians than the tribal language, Mòoré.

Louis heard Walter patiently, and began to weigh his claims against the traditional beliefs of a Mossi upbringing. Could it be possible for the Supreme God, who communed only with spirits, to speak to men like Walter?

What of this claim that the Supreme God had visited the World he'd created, in the person of a man, his second self? Could it be true that he, the Creator, was critical of the state of the hearts of men and women and viewed that state as in utter rebellion against his vision for them, his values and his culture? Was it possible that unless set free from their captivity to evil they and all under their leadership were destined to remain selfishly depraved and incapable of becoming all that the Creator had dreamed for them? Finally, the Supreme God's second self promised the coming of a third self, the same Supreme God, this time in the form of a Spirit. Was it plausible that the Spirit's presence would empower a man or woman to overcome evil within their life and work, to overpower all created spirits opposing them, and to collaborate with them to work for justice and order on behalf of and in cooperation with the civilized world of the Supreme Creator God, re–establishing his Kingdom on Earth as in Heaven?

Walter Lee had explained that it was possible for a man or woman to act on the claims of the second person of God, by determining to change their behaviour; demonstrating unselfishness. Declaration of allegiance to the Supreme God came by symbolic immersion in water. A genuine welcome and a heart warm to relationship would gladly be accepted as home to the third person of God who would bring with him the supernatural power and the divine nature of the Creator himself.

Louis had been intrigued by the possibility of this divine spirit restoring firstly the person, and then all within the limit of their leadership, to civilized life as understood from the perspective of Heaven, the place where the God's first and second self currently lived.

Louis had looked at his compound where his naked children played, taking care to avoid his eye and well clear of his quick fist and harsh words. His young wife made the best of carrying out the work he required of her, her love for him slowly dying as he abused his power over her. He regarded his dusty street where dead dogs lay unburied until the crows and vermin picked their bones clean, and everywhere ramshackle dwellings contained human misery and filth. He was the chief and this was his world. Surely there was a better way.

He was tempted by these fine words of Walter's. A young chief, keen to make a name for himself, he certainly approached the matter with mixed motives. He was to learn in future years this was the case for most human beings encountering the Living God. Each began the relationship in much need of a revolution of motives.

Now it so happened that a few days after his most profound conversation with Walter Lee, Louis prayed for the first time. It was late in November, a crucial time for his crops and those of the village; harvest time was just a few weeks away. The young and vigorous Louis was at the stage of life when he would work his land himself. No sons were yet strong enough to help him, nor indeed to take on the hardest work for him. He was a comparatively expert farmer and his crops stood proudly in good order, well maintained and strong. However the weather looked angrily unsettled and Louis was concerned. He had once as a child witnessed weather like this when a severe wind storm had wrecked his father's crops causing a year's hardship to the family such that he had lost two siblings in the famine that ensued.

A significant storm was forming near enough to be a problem, and the traumatic weather pattern he had observed a child was so etched on his memory that he knew he faced a similar problem himself right now. Compelled by some intuitive prompt, he walked to the edge of his land and watched the storm form before his eyes. The clouds towered into the African sky, coloured orange white at their tops, high and billowing. Lower, towards the nearby hills, the cloud colour turned dark slate grey, an angry moody darkness lit now and then by flashes of lightning. The storm would come, and it had the power to devastate his harvest. Unformed millet heads would lie beside their snapped stalks, rotting where they fell, useless except for animal feed, and then only for a few weeks.

The slow distant weather formation had advanced steadily towards Louis, seemingly gathering in pace as it came. An eerie light and unearthly stillness altered his surroundings giving a spiritual as well as physical feel to the natural phenomenon.

A thought occurred to Louis as he watched the now onrushing storm. What if it really is possible to communicate directly with the supreme God as Walter had suggested? Would he if asked, in the person of his third self, intervene in this extreme emergency? He decided to test the matter.

'Creator God, if you are as Walter has said, send your third self, the one Holy Spirit and command this storm to submit to your authority.' He expected some external force of gigantic proportion to manifest itself and contend with the storm.

Instead something truly remarkable but altogether quite different happened. A fierce anger came upon him, a terrible passionate force of will that rose up from deep inside his being, a part of his person that he knew to be his own — yet until now not active or, he supposed, not fully alive. He found himself commanding the storm as one might speak to an unfamiliar aggressive dog and overpower it by force of will and unflinching uncompromising authority: 'You will not come here! You will not touch my land!' he cried in his own nerveless, authoritative voice.

Unbelievably, the storm broke before his eyes, dividing to the right and to the left of his land. He could see the power of it, but felt nothing of its force. For a period of perhaps 20 minutes it passed his fields, and those of his village, leaving his crops untouched.

As with so many averted crises, the overwhelming fear of potential consequences and worst case scenarios immediately dissipated and was quickly replaced by the normality of work and the return of ordinary emotions. However something had undeniably happened which he could not explain in terms of his own spheres of reference or traditions. He sighed with inexpressible whirling thoughts, and focused on things he did understand: clearing weed and checking his grain for progress towards harvest, and gathering wood for the fire.

On return to the village however Louis found things were very much impacted by the storm as he had feared. His neighbours, those from the villages around had suffered devastating losses to their crops. As Louis ran and walked through the fields of his peers and friends the significance of the transaction that had passed between him and the supreme God of whom Walter had spoken began to clarify in his mind.

It was one week later that Louis was baptized, in the river, before all the people of his village. He publicly burned his fetish stating that he had no need to appease or persuade spirits to do his bidding, he would relate directly to the supreme Creator God himself. He declared that he would share his harvest with those from the villages nearby in need as a result of the storm damage, encouraging his fellow villagers to do the same. From now on he would seek to shape his life in response to one whose leadership was loving, gentle and humble. He told the story of the storm and his own encounter with the authenticity of the deity that lay behind the words of Walter Lee.

'Without the power they are just words,' Louis declared. 'With the power comes a responsibility to respond, I have no choice but to yield, and then to collaborate for all of our futures, and although I have the authority according to our traditions to command you to follow my choice, I release you to make your own.'

Walter Lee preached a sermon full of invitation and inclusion, offering to all who would respond the opportunity to participate in recreating a renewed and better society where behaviour towards fellow men and women was accountable to an unseen but all powerful Creator God. Many from the village were baptized alongside Louis and land was set aside for a place to worship, first beneath the trees, later in a small building constructed by the worshippers.

There were however some, especially those with a vested interest in the traditional worship system, who violently opposed what was happening in Yarbo. It was not long before Louis received a visit from Malidoma, the most powerful shaman in the area, a man greatly to be feared. He came with several other notable shamans. Together they represented a fearsome spectacle. Until the recent transformational events Louis would have been terrified at the thought of such a visit.

Now, however, convinced in his own mind of the doctrinal folly that lay ingrained in the traditional worship culture, itself derived from who knows where and from which influence, he did not fear these men or their spirits.

33

The ultimatum came quickly and simply, pronounced by Malidoma: 'Louis Oudraogo, you will die before next harvest time.'

At 91 years, Louis Oudraogo had already lived to be the oldest man ever in Koloko district. He had buried each of those shamans, every one of his peers and many of their sons. It was as if the Creator God was making a statement, establishing something important. Louis had become a living demonstration of authentic power, and even his enemies moved carefully around the authority he carried.

It was not long before Louis and Walter began to receive invitations from neighbouring villages, particularly those that had received kindness from Yarbo's villagers after their harvests were ruined. They had heard tell of families transformed by this three person God. Of wives no longer beaten, and of old disputes settled by forgiveness. Of generosity, and of a resistance to the fear instilled by the shamans. They wanted churches; could Louis and Walter send someone to build them?

Louis sent his two oldest sons off to the Pentecostal Bible College at Ouagadougou as soon as it was established, and they in turn became powerful pastors then administrators in what rapidly grew to be the largest growing most vibrant spiritual movement the country had ever seen. There had been many spectacular incidents across the territory in those days, and the story of Yarbo was just one in a dazzling array of spiritual illuminations.

The nation had changed unbelievably during his lifetime. The cessation of French colonial rule in the region had seen French Sudan become Mali and with the coup led by the 'African Che Guevara', Thomas Sankara; Upper Volta had become Burkina Faso. The new name meant 'Upright Man' in Mòoré, an indication of the new wind of anti–corruption blowing in the wake of the desperate times after independence from France which had provoked the coup.

• • •

Eve was hungry to hear what the old man had to say, and hurried to get to church early so she could find a place near the front with the other younger unmarried women.

Louis Oudraogo sat to speak. He was an extremely humble and likeable man. He first thanked the church in Djigouera for welcoming him, stating that this was the last time he could make the journey here. His old bones were becoming too troublesome for travelling, but he said he was thrilled to be there and to notice the many families that had chosen to become part of the church. He commended Philippe and Florence for their leadership, and for the able leadership team they had built.

He joked about his infirmity, referring to his own old age being a blessing that gave him the opportunity to enjoy arthritis and rheumatic pain for longer than most. His tone hardened a little as he mentioned in passing those hucksters and charlatans now peddling the gospel message for profit in churches up and down the country, who promised that God healed all diseases and infirmities, and that just having faith would drive these things away.

'Why, Jesus himself healed many, and they're all dead now,' he intoned in his slow gravelly old man voice.

> 'Sickness and death will greet you soon enough and maybe God will do something special for your body and maybe he won't. His interest is in your ability to produce justice and righteousness and to meet the needs of the downtrodden and the oppressed. If he blesses you along the way, well enjoy it, but if you engage with him for your own ends, you have already started badly. I guess that's a little harsh, maybe most of us start out that way, but we need to pretty soon grow out of it. That is the way of discipleship. Build churches if you must, but "make disciples" is his command. It all needs to be about his business anyways, and that business is justice and righteousness.'

Louis went on to talk about eradicating bitterness from your soul.

'It's a killer, your enemy's best weapon against you, right there in your own heart, inside your guard. The only way you'll rip it out of there is to grant the forgiveness your enemy does not deserve, and to be gracious to the ungracious; to overcome evil with good.'

As she listened to the words, made all the more powerful because of their source, Eve felt a strengthening of resolve to face her issues in the reality of life within her own compound.

After the service the congregation enjoyed one another's company. This was when Eve most enjoyed being part of church. Here she was valued. Here she mattered. This was a family she had chosen, not an accident of birth.

Florence tugged at her arm. She wore her usual huge smile beneath her floral navy and cream hat complete with netting and feathers. Perfect hair flowed beautifully from beneath the hat. She was a picture of health and serenity. The younger women all called her mama or aunty, depending on the closeness of the relationship. Eve called her mama, and loved her.

'How are you, child?' When Florence said 'child' it sounded like a precious endearment.

Eve smiled, 'I am well mama.'

'And how is your lovely mother?'

'She is not well mama,' a tear formed in the corner of Eve's eye, 'I fear she will not live much longer.'

'Hush child, have strength. Let me come and pray with her.'

'I would like that.'

'Then we will make it happen, *cherie*, and in the meantime, I need you to take care of something for me.'

She handed Eve a paper bag containing a brightly coloured simple shift dress, made of tough durable cotton. The patterned material from which it was made was woven not printed thus it would stay vivid for as long as the garment lasted.

'I am too big now for such a dress, and it's such a shame for it not to be worn. Wear it for me; let the world enjoy its colour!'

Eve's own dress was a plain indiscriminate muddy grey colour, any pattern long faded away. As her figure had begun to fill out with the development of adult changes, despite her slightness, it was becoming too tight, and there was no obvious way of replacing it. Florence had been observing the child with concern from a distance for some time. With her mother losing her mind, the other women in the household more interested in their own children and her father too caught up in his own vices and problems to take an interest, she was a case of serious neglect. Florence had picked out the dress from a pile of clothes dropped in by an American missionary who had the experience to allow clothing distribution to be handled by the local church rather than succumbing to her own feel-good desires and distributing clothes to a jostling crowd of bumsters — as was sadly so often the case with Western visitors.

Eve was almost overcome by the generosity of the older woman, and impressed by her wisdom, which was immediately apparent to her. If the garment was not Eve's it could not be taken from her. There were other more senior women in the family and that was a very real possibility. It was too small for the owner, so there was no point in her keeping it at her house; Eve felt she would be doing Florence a favour by wearing it for her and giving her pleasure whenever she saw it.

Her happy heart sang for joy as she skipped her way home, but some heaviness returned as she entered the compound and immediately went about her chores as if the morning's service had never happened.

'What's that you've got child?' Dina asked, quick to notice any resource entering the family home.

37

'Mama Florence has asked me to wear a dress for her. It is hers, but she wants me to wear it so she can enjoy it on me.'

Dina seemed satisfied with the explanation and lost interest in the package. Her interest would return soon enough when she saw how breathtakingly beautiful it made Eve look, but that moment could wait, and the principle of ownership had been established. In any case Dina was the size of a house, being so heavily pregnant, and her own daughters were too small to make a claim on the garment.

Later in the day Florence dropped by to visit Mariam. 'Oh *ma cherie*, what has become of you?' She wailed, overcome by compassion and horror at the emaciated vacant crone that had only months earlier been a vibrant and loving mother.

She sat with the dribbling Mariam for half an hour, gently stroking her hair and sharing a bottle of cold water. Mariam drank a little and seemed quiet and stilled by Florence's care. Florence prayed with her, called Eve, who had been busy elsewhere in the compound, gave her a hug and left. Eve could not have adequately expressed what that visit meant to her.

In fact had there been any medical education in the village a few simple tests would have established that Mariam was the victim of vitamin B12 deficiency, a condition easily treated if caught early, though at her stage irreversible. Mariam had for months been sacrificing her own food in favour of her children. Fish, vegetables, even goats milk had gone onto the children's plates. Mariam's diet had been largely cereal and water for too long, and those in small quantities. Initially dizziness and fatigue, apparent deafness due to tinnitus a bit of hair loss dry flaky skin all seemed fairly minor. She had then become unnaturally irritable and subject to uncharacteristic mood swings. Then had come the fainting and extreme fatigue, then loss of concentration and now mental incoherence.

Mariam was about to become another contribution to an unacceptable statistic of life expectancy in Burkina Faso, linked directly to a lack of education and a high level of poverty. For the compilers of statistics she was another figure to add. In fact, there were no statistics for her area and Mariam's passing was recorded nowhere. She was 31 years old.

For Ibrahim there was one less mouth to feed, giving him just enough reserve to make the following harvest with no more famine losses. Mariam had been largely useless, and something of a burden on the others for months. While he still had some feelings for her, their marriage had been very much a working arrangement from the beginning and any emotional attachment to her diminished years ago. He shed no tears.

There was no sense of a happy, peaceful ending to her life; only the grinding downward spiral of a poor woman's death. Ibrahim's meagre resources had not been enough to cover his own appetites, his life choices and his liabilities. Mariam's personal sacrifice in deference to her children's needs had been the ultimate one. Nobody would ever know that, but it was true all the same.

Eve was devastated by the death of her mother. At the funeral Florence's husband, the Reverend Philippe Oudraogo, grandson of Louis spoke of her devotion to Ibrahim. Eve's mind flew back to the night when Ibrahim brought home Dina as his new wife. She saw again in her memory the look of utter indignation disgrace and despair Mariam had worn as she did her best to welcome a dazzling 15–year–old rival into the family. Then had come the indignity of the brutal reorganizing of the sleeping arrangements and the duties, the new wife's scathing deference turning slowly and surely into a mutually supportive alliance of fellow suffering. Even within that there had been the constant bickering over children, food allocation and the few possessions owned by the family.

And finally there had come Bintou, an added misery for both senior wives. Bintou was as expected very much younger and more attractive and had yet to fall out of favour with Ibrahim. She was unbelievably lazy, expecting to be treated like a favourite daughter rather than a fellow wife. Ibrahim had failed to sort this out, even up to today enthralled by Bintou's beauty and very pleased to have got her as his own.

Mariam had died too tired and too incapable to be concerned any longer about internal justice in the family. She did however leave one thing of value to Eve and her other children: relationship with the local Pentecostal church.

Eve lay in the darkness that night in her old tattered dress on her little patch of earth in the crowded house, the new one hung up nearby. Her sisters pressed against her and her brothers snoring nearby, she did something inspired by old Louis Oudraogo. She prayed what was for her a different kind of prayer:

'Creator God, I have been told you are my perfect father in Heaven. To be honest I believe that because I want to believe it. In my life so far I have not seen for myself any evidence that you are there. I long for the day when things on Earth are as I am told they are in Heaven. I guess there is nobody hungry there and that you do not beat your children or get moody.

'I can see that it will not be long now before my father arranges for me to marry a man like himself. I will become as my mother was, and my daughters will grow to be like me. They will marry men who will abuse and harass them mercilessly and who would marry other women to shame and disgrace them. If you are there and you hear my prayer, will you rescue me from this endless struggle please? If you do this I give you my word that I will come back for girls like me and rescue them, I will try to work for a better future for those you give to my care, amen.

'And God, please make my father happier, amen.'

4.   PREY

Ibrahim was desperate. The death of Mariam had marked the beginning of an awful struggle for the family.

The pressure on grain prices had become an annual event, and though he was smarter than some, he always fell foul of his own weaknesses and sold too much of his grain for cash early in the year. This year famine had come early, and the family was already into its 'not eating every day' routine to last out to harvest. The cash was all used up, all his cards played. He had only his two working cows, both hopefully in calf, remaining.

Bintou's pregnancy had gone well until last week, but yesterday she had complained of pains, and there was an unpleasant discharge. She had been examined a month or so ago at the local clinic in Bambara Nkosu, eight miles from Djigouera. The nurse there had confirmed that all was well and the baby was due in October. It was now late July and there should not be any development of this kind at this stage, even Ibrahim knew that.

He borrowed a friend's hand cart for the journey to the clinic. This was a favour and no money was involved.

Eight miles by cart with a sick pregnant woman had to be planned carefully. Because he truly loved her, Ibrahim himself travelled with Bintou taking his eldest son David, born to Mariam, along with them. They set out on the rough tracks before dawn, to avoid the worst of the heat on the journey. They travelled as gently and carefully as possible arriving just before the clinic opened. There was a long queue of desperate people awaiting attention, each penniless, many very sick indeed. Famine, even artificially induced, produced this crop of human misery every July now.

Where there is prey, there are predators, and Benjamin Traoré was a predator. He had learned the choreography of engagement with Christian mission very early in life. From his perspective he had a simple choice to make. He could continue as a Moslem scratching a living in the dust, or he could get friendly with Christians at a nearby health clinic, make himself useful, attend their church, become a good Christian and see what opportunities that opened up for him. It was a well trod path. The local population had a term for it: 'rice Christian' — and he was careful to dance the dance of genuine Christianity very well indeed.

It had been a successful adventure so far. Originally from Mali he had been schooled by overseas Christian sponsorship. He had gained a scholarship through university med school and become a medical doctor in Senegal, moving to Burkina Faso on placement with 'Light to Africa' a British Christian NGO that ran mobile clinics throughout the border region well beyond the reach and indeed the prying, more educated eyes of those in the cities.

Benjamin was well rewarded by his overseas masters for his work as a practicing field GP. His supplies were never quite adequate for the many and complex conditions that presented, but he was better equipped than most. He had a large white 4x4 which could be seen alongside those of many other embassy and NGO staff outside the better restaurants and massage parlours in the city whenever he was in town.

Though many of the NGOs were committed to provision of healthcare, the city had no effective ambulances. There was however, a good quota of white four wheel drive vehicles at the disposal of NGO staff and their families; just one of many anomalies affecting relationship between the local population and the systems of those who would try to alleviate their suffering.

Having the equipment and the supplies Benjamin needed in order to dispense free emergency treatment was the outworking of one of Light to Africa's values statements:

> 'We will provide our field teams with high quality equipment and adequate emergency medical supplies in order for them to be able to deliver the best possible emergency medical care, free at the point of need to those in areas too remote to access hospitals.'

There was however a problem with delivery and that problem was Benjamin. Left to run his own field team he quickly discovered that his two Christian nurses shared a similar value system to his own. Their allegiance to the Christian faith was primarily a financial one. They had acted as he had. Their baptisms and attendance of church had been their entry point to positions of privilege within the lucrative humanitarian structures operating under the banner of the cross. Any thoughts the three of them had of accountability towards an all seeing supreme Creator God were as ridiculous as the Western garb their pastors wore to conduct the business of church in the African heat.

In their view this profligate Western religion was an incongruity to be taken for as much as possible for as long as it lasted. Benjamin and his team had been charging for their services for years now. His rates were set according to the desperation of the unfortunate that needed him. That was the African way. The market was always set according to the level of the customer's desire.

In terms of medical prowess the reputation of the clinic was excellent. It was also known to be expensive. This latter reputation was not a problem to Benjamin as the Mòoré speaking primarily

Mossi people in need had no direct relationship with the English speaking overseas administrators of the NGO. In fact French was the usual European language learned by the Mòoré, and very few of his customers spoke that. There was therefore no hint to the people that Light to Africa services were supposed to be free of charge for their benefit. It was not difficult to keep parties apart and Benjamin and his nurses lived well.

Ibrahim was hoping that Bintou's problems were relatively minor and that he could come to some arrangement with the clinic. The little family stood in the sun for three hours waiting patiently in line before being called into the dispensary. The place had clean water, electricity from a generator, some basic furniture and screens. Benjamin and his two nurses each worked separately unless anything presented that required them to work in team. They were capable of outpatient operations, which could be fairly major, dispensing medicines and if absolutely necessary arranging transportation to the city for hospitalization.

Upon learning that there were pregnancy complications, the specialist midwifery nurse made her examinations.

'Your baby is dead, there is no heartbeat' she stated bluntly.

Bintou was distraught at the news, and began keening, a very familiar sound in this place and one which left the staff and onlookers unmoved. They had heard it several times this morning for various reasons, all terminal.

Ibrahim comforted his wife and enquired about what should now be done.

'The baby is not in the correct position for delivery and has become swollen within the womb. Normal delivery will not be possible, she will need an emergency caesarean section immediately or she too will die.'

'What would be the cost of the operation?' Ibrahim asked softly, his mind racing to his very limited assets.

Benjamin was summoned to fix the price. 'Including all necessary medicine and dressings, the price will be 70 000 CFA.' — an amount that was roughly equivalent to $200 US. He spoke in a professional, brusque tone which invited no counter offer.

Ibrahim was unable to conceal his anguish and aware of the terrified look in his wife's eyes. He asked to see Benjamin alone in order to discuss the matter out of earshot.

'Boss, I do not have the money.'

'Then do not waste my time, go and bury your wife.'

'I am appealing to you as a man, help me!'

'And I am answering you as a professional. I hear this every day. If you love your wife, bring me the money. If you do not, go and bury her.'

'I have cows that I can sell. I have three daughters aged 11 or more. Each will fetch a fine dowry. I can get you the money.'

'Good, then go and get it, bring it here and I will operate.'

'It will take time to find a buyer for my cows. To arrange a marriage for a girl; this would also take time. There is famine, people have no cash. I can get the money together in a few weeks.'

'Then prepare to bury your wife.'

'Have you no mercy boss?'

'I have none for you farmer.'

'I will speak with the shaman'

Benjamin scornfully regarded the scars on Ibrahim's face. 'I am a Christian, and my tribe is from Mali. I have no fear of your ancestral spirits. In any case if you threaten me I will not operate whether you pay me or not. We will not return to this village until two weeks from today, by which time your wife will be dead. I will say one final time: bring me the money this afternoon or prepare to bury your wife.'

Benjamin was disappointed. He could see from Ibrahim's face that there would be no money from this ragged farmer. He had set his price too high but he had learned that once stated there was no way of reducing a price. If others heard that he could be reasoned with he would spend his whole clinic time haggling with desperate people. If Ibrahim had been an attractive woman, then there might be something she could offer him, but a battered stinking Mossi farmer? Pah! He turned back to his queue, the conversation was over.

Ibrahim could not look at Bintou on the long wretched journey home. She knew. Fever had already begun to make her shake uncontrollably and she whimpered and cried out in fear and pain. In desperate anxiety Ibrahim paced the compound. He was a proud man, too proud to ask for help. For the first time in over 15 years he cried. Not the gentle sniffling of self–pity, but the tearing agonized howling born of the frustration anguish and horror of a man finally confronted by the terrible consequences his own selfish choices.

Ibrahim did not say goodbye to Bintou; unable to summon the strength to be near her to comfort her. His emotional and moral resilience was bankrupt. Dina and Eve did their best to care for her. She was quiet by morning and dead at noon.

Ibrahim buried her. He kept his cows and his daughters, but something in his eyes was lost.

• • •

Eve had for a couple of years been the most functional woman on the property. She was bright and happy, very strong like many Mossi women. Her figure had filled out, her smile with those huge bright brown eyes, transfixing. By all accounts she was lovely. This would normally have been a problem for her as she was already eligible for marriage and there had been several suitors from other families — older men keen to enlarge their brood and take in a fine new young wife.

Ibrahim had not been keen to let her go. She was needed here. The dowry he demanded was therefore too high, and even those inflamed by desire for her could not or would not meet his price.

Church remained the one oasis of joy in Eve's life. She loved singing and swaying with the others to the frantic rhythm of the djembe players. The harmonies of the Mossi worshippers were wonderful, and when Rev. Philippe led the meetings, the presence of God was tangible.

Rev. Philippe was as kind and gentle as his wife Florence. He spoke with passion and compassion. He described a God who cared, and he lived as if he knew him. He had built around himself a team of pastors and worship leaders, both men and women, who together loved and shared life with the people of the villages around the church. They visited the sick and prayed with them. In fact there had been some occasions when undeniably those sick had been made well again. They shared wealth where it was possible to do so, shared clothing and equipment across the compounds. It was a community whose values were genuinely built upon love and forgiveness. The spiritual legacy of old man Oudraogo was in his children's children and he would die one day soon, a happy man at peace with his God, with no outstanding issues against his fellow men. An example, if ever there was one, of a life well lived.

Since the moment of her first real attempt to reach out to God when her mother died, Eve had settled for a more passive relationship. There had been no apparent response despite her genuine and frank appeal to him so Eve supposed he was occupied elsewhere or interested in more important people.

At church there was also the matter of Joseph, Florence and Philippe's son.

Joseph was a tall well set lad of eighteen. He was highly intelligent, with a ready laugh and an easy grace about him which came from being a much loved child. His mother had cared most attentively for him, and his father set a moral and courteous tone to the family which had grounded Joseph well in values which had the chance in future years of leading to a noble character. He was cheeky but not insolent, mischievous but not cruel.

He was one of the few children locally who attended school, and once there kept up with work and achieved the grades, despite some woeful teaching. Education was free, but as with healthcare, free education was laughably undeliverable and every child was expected to make a small payment. Any resources needed by the children had to be provided by their families. Travel to and from school was on foot, and younger children had to be taken by older siblings or parents, which precluded any work in the fields. Most families could not be bothered, and this suited the government as provision of schooling was beyond the national budget even with the assistance of NGOs.

Learning was mainly by rote and classes in the few existing schools were of 70 to 100 children crammed onto little benches. Many children would fall behind in their understanding of lessons. There was no one–to–one support possible in such large classes. They would continue to attend school year after year, chanting enthusiastically, learning nothing.

Both Joseph's parents were literate, and he had considerable support at home, where there was a chalk board. It was usually filled with what Eve observed as unintelligible squiggles, some of which looked like bananas and the outlines of leaves, others like knives and cooking pots.

Eve adored Joseph and to her amazement, over the last year Joseph had begun to show interest in her.

It had begun with him mentioning her name and including her in his circle of friends after church. Then she had caught his eye during a meeting as his hands danced skillfully upon his djembe.

His face lit up as he flashed a delighted smile when she acknowledged his gaze.

Inclusions in group fun, and shared glances became long conversations alone as he walked her home from church. Her full brothers, all three now strapping young men, also church members on account of their mother's influence, loosened their attendance of her and walked respectfully ahead of Eve and Joseph. The two began to spend more time alone together, in full visibility of the family of course, and with the kind of modesty expected of the unusual local blend of traditional Mossi customs and Christian moral values.

Ibrahim took this turn of events in his stride. He could not keep Eve forever. Rev. Philippe and Florence would more than likely have enough substance to provide a respectable dowry. The family was well liked by Mariam's children and had been kind to Eve. He approved of the friendship, and would make no trouble when the time came.

When Joseph was close to Eve he became so inflamed he found it difficult to breathe or to focus on anything other than possessing her. His appetite was fitful and he picked at his food for a time when he was unsure that his interest in her was requited. He could not even contemplate life without this lovely young girl with the beautiful fiery eyes, the dignified strength borne of hardship and suffering, and the laughing softy spoken mouth which he longed to kiss. When she spoke, his spirit was gentled, when she sang his heart ached, when she walked and her hips swayed, all sorts of other things happened to him that he tried desperately not to think about. He was a lost cause, and very happily so.

Joseph was completely convinced of his calling to become a pastor and spoke earnestly about it with Eve. He was pretty convincing as well as being convinced. Eve recognized that if her future was with him, then she may be embracing a life of service to God, which may be one of poverty and difficulty. There were many examples of failed rural churches where the pastor had strived to build a workable congregation then simply given up in frustration and starvation as his little patch of land and meagre collection had failed to meet his own family's needs.

She was aware too that her country held strongly to Islamic and animist traditions. Even the churches that were vibrant and growing had often come into conflict with those of other beliefs. In truth the beliefs were so incompatible that conflict was inevitable.

Eve was from a poor farmer's home, she had no expectations other than becoming the dutiful wife of a poor farmer. For her the opportunity to enter the world of ministry, even with potential disaster ahead was not really a major risk in that she had lived at major risk all her life. There was of course a potential high cost if the decision was wrong but something within her was starting to stir about that one deepest prayer to God. Maybe, just maybe he had heard her.

'I must travel to Ouagadougou to attend the Pentecostal Bible College there. It will be for two years and I will not be able to return home to this church during that time. When I come home I will ask your father for you.'

'I will wait for you.'

And so their commitment to one another was sealed.

• • •

Rev. Philippe Oudraogo was truly angry. He had not felt this way in all the years of his ministry.

His life as a pastor was a window onto the world of the families around him. It was both one of privilege and pain. He was a man of great empathy and compassion, one who would sit late at night in prayer, communing with the fount of all wisdom in order perhaps to gain some slight insight into the complexities and decisions that characterized the lives of his community.

There were many marriage disputes usually over dowries and forced arrangements. In fact if pressed he would say these could be the most difficult of his problems to solve. If he became aware of young people falling in love he was quick to speak with parents to make sure that any arrangements for marriage they were thinking of making fell in line with the natural attractions of their offspring. Experience had taught him that to cut across the strength of two young people's desire for one another with a better plan from the parents was a recipe for unhappiness, and possibly infidelity in the future, or elopement in the immediate.

If a couple could successfully negotiate the obstacles prior to marriage then there were not just petty issues to face afterwards. Generations of brutal wife battering and child beating were very resistant to the writings of the New Testament. He had found that couples resplendent in fine clothes on Sunday sometimes morphed into monsters in the home between meetings. Florence had many times ministered to bleeding women, and indeed some injured men, while he had sat patiently working through deep seated misogyny or the natural reaction to it, manipulation and preemptive striking. Anxieties, fears or regressions that triggered the brutality in the guilty party usually produced remorse and it was his ability to lovingly restore and reconcile through patient hours of painful tearful negotiation that had brought lasting change to many of his families.

Occasionally a crime would be committed, a remark too sharp to be overlooked, a boundary dispute, tittle–tattling about others' dabbling with the shaman, minor perceived injustices and petty fights over the condition of borrowed tools on return. Sometimes he felt like everyone's dad, the villain of the piece when he sided with the unjustly treated, and a miserly skinflint when he presented as no soft touch towards the hungry who had yet to really stretch to help themselves.

Some of these things had aroused his anger. 'The best of men is a man at best.' Nothing however had made him as angry as he was today.

It was a Thursday, the second of the two days per fortnight when the mobile clinic was provided in Bambara Nkosu. Yesterday noon one of his congregants, Eric had run panting into his compound. When they'd given him some water and calmed him down he blurted out that his sister Flora had been taken very sick and that he and his father Franck had carried her to the clinic. On arrival there they had been told that she had acute appendicitis and needed an operation. The operation would cost 5000 CFA in cash. They had no cash, but could probably raise it. The man in charge had been absolutely unmovable. If he was to carry out the operation, he must be paid in cash in advance. Eric was desperate; his sister was going to die. He had run the eight miles back from the clinic in the hope that the church could help.

Franck had been part of the church since a power encounter over the healing of his wife's fever had demonstrated the authenticity of the church's God six years ago. The family had shared what they could with others in need many times in the past.

Philippe knew exactly what he must do. For years now transport had been a problem for him. The church had planted two more congregations, each over ten miles away in different directions. He had appointed pastors, both of whom had struggled and were very much in need of his ongoing support. He also had very many families who travelled considerable distances to his own church. He had weighed the matter, balancing his own desires and the legitimate needs of his ministry, and had decided to ask the church to raise funds for a motor scooter for him. Those funds had reached 9000 CFA, not sufficient yet for the purchase, but clearly well on their way towards enabling it to happen.

Philippe had gone to the small cash box kept at the rear of the church office, removed CFA 5000 and handed the money in a paper bag to Eric. It was possible that the family could repay the church in good enough time not to affect the transport fund, but this was a setback, possibly a test.

Eric was not capable of running the eight miles back to Bambara Nkosu. The task was given to his younger brother Fabrice. Fabrice had made the best time he could, and when he had arrived at the Light to Africa clinic, there were still two more hours of treatment time available. The father, Franck fell to his knees pouring out his thanks to God. He blessed the day he had first met Philippe Oudraogo, rejoiced in the provision of the one he worshipped. The little family pressed forward to the front of the queue. They had already waited long enough.

In the heat, with little water or shade, things had not gone well for Flora. The infected appendix in her abdomen had ruptured and a vicious fever had begun to wrack her body.

Benjamin examined the little girl. What had previously been a simple procedure was now likely to be a total nightmare. He was not even sure he could save her, and he was low on the antibiotics she would need. The clinic was nearing the end of the day and this was one headache he didn't need.

He spoke quickly, quietly, directly and finally as always: 'Her condition is worse, she will need more work. The price will be 10 000 CFA.'

Franck and Fabrice reeled in bewildered shock. The elation they had so recently felt on having secured the funds needed to save Flora's life turned all the more bitter as they realized the desperate situation they now faced.

'Surely there must be some mistake. We have raised the money you requested.'

'There is no mistake, it is now not enough.'

'Brother have mercy, she is just a child. We cannot raise this amount, she will die.'

'I have no mercy for you farmer, now go.'

'You are a devil, may you rot in hell.'

'I am a Christian; I have no fear of hell.'

It was that last statement as reported back to him that had motivated Philippe to act. Flora had died in the night. His 5000

CFA was back in the motorcycle fund tin, and one of his families was in total despair.

Philippe had been present at a pastors' conference in Ouaga only a few months previously. There he had heard a presentation from Sir Ralph Jefferson, head of a British Christian NGO — Light to Africa. The NGO chief spoke through a translator, and Philippe was able to follow him in French. Light to Africa was looking to expand following many successful years of operating in the Mali border regions. It was their hope to strengthen partnership with the Pentecostal movement and use church buildings to extend the provision of free medical care, currently only available in areas of extreme need.

Philippe had been puzzled at the time, hearing that medical services would be free of charge to the needy. That was not his experience. Since he was the only pastor from the areas in which Light to Africa was working, he had been anxious to approach Sir Ralph. However there were very many much more high profile supervisors and pastors at the conference, most of whom could speak a little English. The opportunity did not arise for him to question the Englishman. He had returned to his village with his hopes for clarity unanswered.

The amoral behaviour of Benjamin troubled Philippe. It was clear to him that the man should have some mercy and compassion in the circumstance that had just presented. Philippe had prayed last night, seeking the wisdom of God and the revelation of scripture in order to illuminate his actions. He knew that in the first instance if one brother had an issue with another he should seek a meeting face to face as individuals. If that was not successful in achieving the required behaviour change, he should take a witness along with him, and if there was still no change he should expose the man before the whole church.

As he set out towards the clinic, Philippe prayed over and over that in his anger he would not sin.

Benjamin was busy as always when Philippe arrived. When he stopped for lunch he was a little annoyed that Philippe did not stand in line patiently waiting while he took his break as was his usual expectation of those in need of his services.

He took in Philippe's clothing, immediately and rightly judging him to be a rural pastor, probably of limited means, possibly with a congregant in need of treatment. He would hear the pastor out, he had many times benefitted from the altruistic behaviour of churches towards their congregants' medical costs. He had found that a group could afford far higher fees than an individual family.

'Brother, I call you brother because I see that you work in the context of Christian ministry. I need to take issue regarding an important matter which arose yesterday.'

Benjamin's eyes narrowed. This was an unusual start to the conversation. Philippe outlined the reason for his visit, Benjamin's eyes widened at hearing the matter relayed through a reasonably educated third party's account.

In clear measured tones, Philippe checked with Benjamin regarding how the conversation with Franck had ended, and Benjamin confirmed that he had indeed been called a devil and threatened with hell and no, he didn't take it seriously; in fact he felt his retort hadn't been scathing enough. If that was all Philippe had come to discuss then he was sorry things hadn't turned out better for the farmer and his daughter, but what could he do? He couldn't help everybody and if they couldn't afford him that was their problem.

Philippe reasoned as carefully as he could:

> 'Brother I do believe you are in danger of the fires of hell, and my friend spoke hastily but he spoke the truth, and you should heed his warning. My reason is simple enough. If you had truly stopped your rebellion against God and his Kingdom rule, you would in the years of your development as a Christian, increasingly demonstrate behaviour in keeping with that of God himself. God who requires mercy of his people does not easily overlook behaviour such as yours.

'The scripture clearly indicates that "by their fruit you shall know them" and that fruit throughout scripture is found to be righteousness and justice. My friend in this case you have demonstrated neither, and this is not the first time you have behaved in this way. Two years ago we buried another of my village in similar though not quite such extreme circumstances. It seems there is a pattern of behaviour in you which is at odds with that of the children of God and I am here as a pastor to correct you and offer you the chance of repentance. This is for the benefit first of those in need of your help, and then of you who will in due course answer for acts committed in the name of Christ. I come in love seeking the best for all, including you.'

Benjamin smirked throughout this monologue, averting his gaze and tracing a random pattern on the ground with his sandal. How could this mildly spoken fiercely passionate pastor possibly understand the countless scars that laced his soul from the numerous times he had deprived or exploited the needy? Was the pastor so naïve as to believe in this nonsense about any call the divine might have upon his, Benjamin's life? Look at him in his worn clothes, with work–hardened hands. He clearly worked his own land. He didn't even have a ministry that could fully support him, nor an education as rich and international as Benjamin's. Why he didn't even have a vehicle, and probably had little understanding of nutrition or hygiene. How could he possibly engage this fellow at his level on the subject of his, Benjamin's personal behaviour or matters to do with how he conducted his medicine? He was certainly not about to bare his soul to this hard–eyed stranger with whom he had no relationship and no desire have one.

Benjamin wondered how he could humour Philippe and get rid of him without too much of a scene.

'Pastor, you are wasting your time on me,' he said kindly. 'I hold to the fact that Jesus has saved me, and that He'll be back for me when the time comes. As for now, well this world and the majority of its people will be destroyed soon enough, how I make sense of the time available to me is my business. I make plenty of people well but to what end? Most of them are doomed to hell anyway.'

Philippe was floored by this statement. Their perspectives on Christian doctrine were poles apart. True enough the gospel when simplified to sermonettes could be reduced to the legal niceties of the written arguments indicating that salvation for the human condition was found in Christ alone and that it was a free gift simply requiring acceptance. However, it was also clear that this acceptance was not unconditional, and that entry into new life was the start of what should be an adventurous relationship with the living God.

It should lead to a life of participating in the advance of the justice and righteousness of the Kingdom. It was not as Benjamin was suggesting an insurance against the poor race and selfish finish of one who had continued to live in rebellion against the Kingdom's values and the King's instructions.

There was not time to engage in the pastoral care that in Philippe's opinion Benjamin clearly needed but would not accept. This was not the place, theirs was not the relationship. Instead, out of care for those suffering at his hands Philippe decided to try and bring a last incisive challenge to Benjamin's approach to his work.

'I was in Ouagadougou in the springtime,' he said. 'I heard there Sir Ralph speak about your organization. He said that what you do should be without charge. I want to know if you are authorized to behave in his name as you do.'

It was Benjamin's turn to be floored. His mind reeled at the impact of these words. It was a circumstance which was so unlikely he had pushed any forward planning for it away.

There were of course moments of panic late at night when he was unable to shut out the memories of the faces, particularly their eyes, and the screams of the desperate and the dying. He did wonder at times what would happen if the extent of his behaviour were exposed but this served only to increase his anxiety. Denial, suppression and avoidance had dominated his internal coping strategy.

His entire lifestyle was based around profiteering. It was unlikely now that he could live within his legitimate means. He had two children in school, one in university. He had his second family out here in the borderlands, unknown to his wife, his church and of course his organization. There were his indulgent activities downtown; very expensive and it would be very hard to deny himself such habitual pleasures. There were the fine clothes, his wife's 4x4, his wider family's needs. He had come too far on this journey. He was lost to living within the boundaries of integrity and could never retrace his steps to the simplicity that would be necessary on his salary alone.

He would have to act quickly.

'Pastor, I am authorized on behalf of Light to Africa to dispense healthcare in, according to my judgment, the best and most effective way in this territory. You may check with whomsoever you wish, in the meantime, I have my lunch to take, and then patients to attend to.'

Philippe returned home saddened, defeated and puzzled by the doctor. He would take the matter up with his supervisor, maybe go and visit the clinic again with him as a witness.

The powerful off–road motorcycle came to the church a few days later. Two men, Malian by the sound of them, asked to see the pastor, their heads and faces covered against the dust by brightly coloured bandanas. Philippe greeted them warmly, slightly surprised that they had not taken off the cloths covering their faces. The smaller one drew an automatic weapon from his holdall and fired two bursts. The first burst destroyed Philippe's face replacing his handsome smiling features with bloodied smashed bone. The second mangled his chest, leaving his ribs scythed open; his heart still.

The men quickly left the village, cloth masks still in place, the bike bearing no license plates.

• • •

Louis Oudraogo conducted the funeral. For most of the service he remained seated.

'I thought I had spoken in this church for the last time, it seems life has taken an unexpected turn and I am here again.' The old man could not restrain a tear from slowly making its way from the corner of his eye, down over the many creases and laughter lines, to the corner of his mouth.

'A man should not have to see his grandson's funeral and today is a sad one for us all, especially it seems, for me.'

He took a pause for composure.

'Philippe was a good man, many here can testify to that. However it is not in the strength of the many good things he has done that he stands now in the presence of Almighty God. Those good things are merely the evidence of the legitimacy of a transaction he made with his Creator in my home when he was just a little boy.

'He accepted the leadership of Jesus Christ, God's second self, who in the form of a man was the only one capable of getting the show back on the road after humankind chose to rebel against him, and chose Hell over Heaven. Philippe knew, even at that early age, his need of a Saviour to deal with the fact that he was rotten to the core like the rest of us. And he lived his life experiencing the transforming power of God's third self in his own heart, making good what was rotten, bringing to vibrant life what was not.

'You see my friends, Hell is life on your terms. You make yourself God, you construct systems that behave as if they are God, you set up structures that ignore or worse deliberately defy the very source of life itself, and as sure as the sun is hot, you will spend your life on Earth attempting to live in Hell, and when your life here ends you will get your wish and go there.

59

'However, invite the source of all life to become the centre of your life and God's Kingdom will transform you and transform your world into something a little bit more like the future. And the future my friends, is the Kingdom of God, of that I am increasingly certain. All other kingdoms will ultimately fail, every other system will cease.'

He looked at the packed front four rows on which sat the church's grief stricken leadership team and Philippe's distraught family. Then he addressed the coffin: 'My son's son, as with your master, your success will be with your successors.'

He looked again at the front row. 'It is over to you little children, over to you.'

'And now there is a piece of business that needs to be taken care of, just in case I myself fail over something about which I have advised and cautioned you for many years.

'One of the first of the great missionary disciples was born in a tragedy such as this. Steven, a promising, powerful young leader lost his life at the hands of merciless men who could not live with his goodness so they cut him down.

'As he died he showed his killers his final piece of evidence that his heart had been transformed by his master, and he released them from responsibility to him before God for what they were doing to him.

'One of those killers, in fact the one who oversaw the mob that carried out the violence against him, was very soon afterwards making his own peace with God, transforming in due course into the great missionary, Paul the Apostle. You could say Paul got Steven's role in God's Kingdom becoming in due course the most powerful and most promising of the next generation of leaders.'

Louis coughed and paused, gathered himself as if preparing for a titanic struggle.

'I'm guessing Philippe never got the chance, so as the senior man in our family I'm going to do it for him.'

Another cough.

'I formally release from the responsibility to answer to me or my family before God for their crimes, the killers of my grandson and anyone who stood behind them, whatever their motive. I call on almighty God to have mercy on them.'

The old man stood, leaning, trembling on his battered stick and led the congregation in praying for the souls and for the blessing of those who had killed Philippe.

He would die an old man with no bitterness, no regrets.

5.   POOR

'I will not eat this crap! I want fries, I want pizza, I wanna hamburger, anything, just don't feed me this crap.'

Candice was embarrassed. She could think of a few hundred places she would rather be than here on a camp site in the hills above the Mexican city of Tijuana listening to the whining teenage tantrum of a spoilt brat, especially in the presence of hosts.

For one thing it was cold, really cold. Secondly she had bought an economy sleeping bag at the last minute from Target. Casper had begged her to let him take her to Bass Pro, but she'd heard it was some kind of a shrine to blood sports and it really hadn't appealed to her. Casper hadn't been too disappointed; he had arranged to take Chip there while she was away. Chip was coming down to stay while she was on the mission trip, in fact he'd arrived last night and had already begun to put his inimitable stamp on things. The apartment reeked of smoke after they'd tried to use some portable barbecue contraption out on the balcony and everything had got out of hand. Cries of 'I can't see, I can't see!' and, 'fire in the hole!' had wafted in from the balcony and billowing smoke had set off the alarms. They'd had a lovely time.

Yesterday morning after Casper had dropped her off in the Lexus she had noticed a pair of brass testes dangling from the rear bumper. Casper had waved gaily; oblivious of the hilarity his sensational departure was provoking. It looked like being a long week for him and she smiled at the thought of Chip's irrepressible personality lighting up the place, possibly literally.

She'd not smiled much since. The kids had decorated the convoy of rental vans with 'dry wipe' marker pens. This was fun until Buzz had noticed an inappropriate word and attendant 'up arrow' scrawled rather naughtily in large wobbly block letters on the outside of his driver's door. It was then that they realized the marker pens were permanent ones, and the team of leaders was wondering how they could get the necessary solvents down into Mexico in time to remove the art work before the vans went back. There were nine vans involved, it was no small task.

Buzz's door decoration had unfortunately wrecked the first scenes of the video they were making in which he'd made a neat speech about the aims of the trip to camera through his open driver's window. Immediately below his earnestly animated face was emblazoned the word PENIS. 'Take two,' Candice murmured to herself. Buzz was annoying and was already showing her the kind of attention that made her apprehensive about working closely with him for the five day trip ahead.

Passing through the border, something Candice had never done, was a shock. Despite the fact that they were less then 20 miles from her home in the Bay, she felt like she had entered another world.

Graffiti was daubed on every building near the main road. Miles and miles of cobbled together shacks clung impossibly to the hillsides. Someone in her van pointed out that when the rains came some of these canyons became unstable and whole settlements could wash away in minutes.

Each shack represented God knows how many people. The sheer scale of the desperately inadequate housing appalled her. She simply could not process what she was seeing but she couldn't shut it out either. She stared open mouthed as the little convoy passed close to the informal communities served by dirt tracks.

Before long they were passing through the gates of a remote camp site and dumping kit and luggage around a group of small canvas cooking tents and serving areas. In the distance she saw a line of portable toilets of the kind used on building sites, only older. She shuddered. She had heard about them from people who'd done this before.

They were sleeping in tents purchased for the trip by the church and those tents were a nightmare. All the kids objected to the sleeping arrangements which had been drawn up at the last minute by Buzz according to alphabetical order and gender. There were loads of tantrums and a massive row during which Buzz, overwhelmed by the multiple calls on his decision making and criticisms of his actions, completely lost his temper.

The tent pegs would not go into the ground, despite it being wet and slimy on top owing to the cold wet weather on the day they were put up. The weather here had apparently been roasting hot for the last two weeks and it had baked hard underneath. There were only three hammers and one air bed pump between 20 tents and 57 air beds. Nobody would share and everyone was shouting, especially Buzz, who was starting to look like something of an organizational Muppet.

Finally, after an epic struggle with the camp site, a welcome meeting around a roaring fire, a hot chocolate and a visit to the toilets the combination of which had had left her exhausted, traumatized and emotional, she had got into her budget sleeping bag and attempted to freeze herself to death. By morning she was wearing all her clothes, could not feel her feet, and despite needing to relieve herself could not contemplate doing so until the camp fire thawed her out.

Buzz had opted for the mission provider's 'authentic Mexican food' cuisine. This had the triple advantage of giving everyone a deeper understanding of Mexican food (which Buzz loved), it was cheaper, and Buzz didn't have to arrange anything himself.

This decision was the root cause of this morning's tantrum from Taylor. 'It's shit,' she pronounced, 'my mom will be mad when she finds out you tried to make me eat it.'

'I don't appreciate that kind of language. It's perfectly agreeable cactus omelette, your mom isn't here, and if she was I'm sure she would encourage you to eat it.'

'It's shit, shit, shit, shit, shit, shit, shit!'

'Now that's enough! If you want my help you can stop using that language and start acting like you agreed to when you signed up for the trip.'

Taylor stopped cursing and brightened a little at the prospect of Candice possibly offering some help. She had found at home that the more god-awful fuss she made the more her mom and dad would eventually back down. Candice was going to be a pushover.

It was still barely daylight and the breakfast team; made up mainly of bustling Mexican women with an Ablaze leader plus a few kids from the Ablaze group were just becoming visible in the half light. Candice approached the mission provider's overseer, also on duty, an absolutely lovely woman by the name of Sarah. Originally from Alaska, she'd come down to help one summer and somehow gone on to sow her life into serving mission trip teams here in Tijuana ever since. She really was the sweetest gentlest woman Candice had met.

'Well, if she really can't eat it I can see what we have in the trailer,' offered Sarah. 'There might not be much but I'll see what I can do.'

As she turned toward the trailer a group of kids who'd picked up on the possibility of an alternative to cactus omelette came running over. The largest mouth in the group spoke first. 'Hey Chica, watcha got for us?'

'Watch you manners, Sarah is an Alaskan, she is just wearing a Mexican apron.' Candice felt the need to steer the group towards decorum. She was on a loser there.

'Hey Sarah Palin, go shoot us a moose! We're starving!' There was laughter, scathing rather than friendly. 'Yeah Palin, catch us some proper food, not this crap!'

Sarah looked a little taken aback. She would not treat anyone so unkindly herself and didn't really know how to respond. Instead she busied herself with fetching something from the trailer. She returned with a box of cookies meant to form part of their packed lunch and there was a mad scramble from the group of kids, each grabbing as many as they could, dispersing as soon as the whole box was empty.

'Sorry,' said Candice, 'I guess they're a little over–excited.'

'Oh that's alright, I do understand. They're always like this when they first get here, they'll get settled in soon enough once they all start working together on the house.'

Somehow the whole group struggled its way through the process of making its own packed lunch, eating egg and cactus, drinking coffee, filling water containers, applying sun block and loading up the vans for day one of the action.

• • •

At the work site they were introduced to the Mexican family led by Pablo and Daniella who were all very shy and unnerved, particularly the children. Candice would make a special effort with them. Building was not her thing, but shy children? Well that was more her line. A dazzling smile and simple welcoming body language were all the introductions needed. Before long they were enjoying one another's company chattering away to each other with no common language except giggles and gestures. Children she could do.

Day one was absolutely shattering. For the first hour, mainly hand carrying things around the site and arranging equipment, laying out pieces of wood, holding discussions with the family about the positioning of doors and windows and stowing kit safely away from the work areas made things busy and fairly straightforward.

Their build site team of 17 people, predominantly comprised of older teenagers included a few veterans of previous trips. It also included Phil, their highly experienced build site manager, a church member who was in construction.

The sun came out and the temperature soared. The work quickly changed from shifting stuff around to full scale chain gang attrition. The team first had to dig out a load of rocks from the area designated for the house's concrete foundation slab. Then they needed to level the ground, including building up one corner with the rocks they'd removed from elsewhere. These needed to be smashed up with club hammers. Finally there was a trench to dig all around the edge of the slab, and then hand mixing and pouring tons of concrete for the slab itself. The final product of their labour was a concrete foundation and floor cut into the ground and shaped like an upside down shoe box lid.

After seven hours in the heat, forcing everyone to drink, spraying them with cold water, applying and re-applying sun block, buying sombreros for the whole team from the street traders, and doing her share of the graft, Candice was frankly wrecked.

Over lunch she'd won over the children in the Mexican family. It had cost her half her lunch, but she didn't eat usually eat much anyway.

Four more days of this? Not sustainable surely? She was an athlete, absolutely used to iron discipline, hard work, getting back on form after injury, dealing with hunger and thirst. In this context she was one gritty girl, and certainly the best performer apart from Phil, who had really hit his stride. She had however got very dirty, something that hadn't happened to her in over 15 years. She felt very strange indeed looking at what were undoubtedly her jeans caked in concrete, her arms smeared with mud and cement dust, Ugh.

Taylor had spent her day alternately whining and sulking. With only 17 on the team there was nowhere to hide, and her desultory efforts were starting to grate on her fellow builders. She was under a deal of peer pressure and was forced to re-evaluate Candice who had turned out to be a cross between Superwoman and Neytiri from Avatar.

Blair, the founder and C.E.O. of the trip provider was detailed to be with their team today. He was a long way from any picture Candice may have had of a founder and C.E.O. If anything he reminded her of Chip. Early in the day he had begun winding up Phil with messages purporting to be from Buzz.

At 11.30 a.m.: 'Buzz says his team has nearly finished its slab already and his people are wondering about doing another one just for fun.'

Phil, responding very well to the genre came back with, 'Tell Buzz that it's supposed to be more than 2cm thick. He's gonna need to dig it all out and start again.'

'Buzz says your team couldn't mix a cake, leave alone a foundation slab.'

'Tell Buzz he'll have great difficulty eating anything other than soup by the time we've finished with him.'

And so on back and forth all day.

Around mid afternoon, having dropped off a particularly well aimed jibe from 'Buzz' Blair, backing away from the site hooting with mirth at his witticism went backwards over a wheelbarrow handle that took him perfectly behind the knees. All hands downed tools and roared with laughter at him. Blair roared along with them.

Somehow this hilarious man had just the right touch to lift everyone's spirits through the tough hours. They sensed a person full of life. He was good to be around, as in fact was everyone on his nonprofit organization's team.

Candice liked Blair, and found him approachable.

'You will not believe how cold I was last night.'

'Budget sleeping bag huh?'

'Yeah I guess.'

'We had one guy come down here one year who was so cold he urinated into his water bottle and cuddled it to warm himself up.'

'You don't say?'

He grinned and she playfully punched him, thinking she'd been had. Nobody would be nuts enough to do that surely! Or would they? He'd seemed believable!

Blair wandered off chuckling, looking for another leg to pull.

Phil called the build site team together at the end of the day.

'Ladies and gentlemen we have completed the slab. As I told you this morning, completion of the overall build on time depends to a great extent on accomplishing this task on day one. You have achieved it. We are on track. Well done.'

There was a burst of applause and some cheering. The team piled into a couple of vans, hands blistered, limbs sore but spirits soaring. They sang Motown on the way back, Candice leading the girls in a sing–off against Phil and the lads. For the first time in a long time, the half dead Candice began to feel truly alive.

Back at camp, it was time to shower. Candice and the other girls picked up their hand filled camp showers which had been lying out all day in the sun. They headed towards the whitewashed shower block in their bathing costumes and flip flops. There was some hilarity going on in the men's block. There was an English group in and apparently nobody had told one of the leaders he needed to wear swimming trunks in the showers thus he was the only one naked. Whoops and hollers and heavily accented cries of, 'Watch out for the pervert!' and, 'Somebody cover that up!' carried easily into the women's area provoking smiles and snickers — boys!

Showering was not easy. The bags were fitted with a pipette–like tap that emitted a feeble stream not dissimilar to that produced by a small male dog at a fire hydrant. It knocked off the worst of the caked dirt but the equipment wasn't really up to the task of washing hair.

After showering, a bit of down time was followed by the main meal.

La Cocina, the Mexican in–camp food provider, gave them lightly spiced beef steak cut into strips, marinated until wonderfully aromatic and tasty, and presented in crunchy tubes of savoury corn biscuit, garnished with soured cream and served with salad. There was an excited buzz around the food area, where everyone sat around on canvas chairs hungrily eating the wonderful fare provided. An appreciative quiet settled over the team and those who wanted more, which was everyone, received second and indeed third helpings.

Well fed, the group enjoyed its first real whole team spiritual meeting, and was introduced for the first time to the other half of the nonprofit's C.E.O. team, a small Texan woman, incredibly bright eyed and with that battle hardened kind of toughness which cannot be faked; softened by years of experience of helping complete newbies into combat.

'The grave is empty' began the small Texan woman. She spelled out a lifetime of commitment to the Mexican families around the border regions and to the churches that sought to reach out to them with the love of Christ.

'I kept my promise to the little boys and girls in that Tijuana dump orphanage. I said that somehow I would come back and build homes for their families so they could live with their parents again.' she concluded to stunned silence. There was not a dry eye among the team.

Her account had taken them through stories of people living in cars, who had never dreamed of owning a waterproof secure home, those living under tarps, bringing up children diseased, soaked and frozen in the winter times. She recounted a life story which had so far seen 17 000 families housed in appropriate homes through the mobilizing of hundreds of thousands of generous members of church youth teams. The breathtaking scale of the social justice she had been engaged in for over 30 years was undeniably impressive.

She declared that the empty grave of a man executed by an empire was the start of a Kingdom whose power came from love and forgiveness not weapons and bullying. She described it as unstoppable kingdom whose entry point was humility and whose advance was irresistible. Death could not overcome it, human empire could not defeat it; both of these giants would one day bow before the owner of that empty grave.

Candice had never before seen so clearly the emptiness of her largely pagan Christian existence. The little woman had spoken of a journey of discipleship, of self-denial. She had alluded to a kingdom of justice whose citizens increasingly understood the importance of what its King had to say, and gladly shaped their lives in obedience to him. There was no political rhetoric, no railing against anyone, or praying for things to fall into line with personal interests; just a simple obedience to meet needs and contend against injustice by direct action. All this compelled by the passion of the one to whom the downtrodden prayed.

After the meeting she observed Blair at pace carrying a soccer ball, being pursued by a howling mob of English teenagers. As she watched he ran into a trailer hitch and for the second time in a day lay in the dust surrounded by laughing kids. This was an altogether different kind of leadership from anything she had known. Her forehead puckered into a rather pleasing little frown as she tried to make sense of something wonderful concealed in plain sight all around her. She sensed it was about values and was becoming excited about discovering what they might be.

In her sleeping bag that night, Candice lay double wrapped in Mexican blankets purchased from the onsite store whose profits supported the local churches. She reflected on the difference this epic day had made to her perspective. She was shattered emotionally, physically, mentally. And for the first time in years she was beginning to realize why she was not at peace.

Speaking of peace, knowing that she was on breakfast duty at 4.30 a.m. the following morning, she had turned in at 9.00 p.m. only to find that the English group; gathered in a kind of circus tent close by on the site were singing lustily. She eventually drifted off to an endlessly repeated semi tuneless rendition of Bill Withers' 'Lean on me'.

• • •

Day two on the work site involved a completely different set of skills, and a bunch of splinters. She spent the day plying tweezers and when not calling on her first aid skills, trying to saw and hammer nails straight; two skills that had eluded her life up until this point.

Her relationship with the Mexican children, Cesar and Daniela was a highlight. They had one toy between them, an old doll with one missing arm possibly something discarded they had picked up. Their home was a cobbled together shack of ill fitting planks and old garage doors. She had slipped inside a few times to collect items for the new build which were stored in there. Everything was covered in dust. There was an old sofa, colourless, ripped shapeless and stinking. A kitchen table piled high with odds and ends, bits of cloth and some battered plates and spoons, stood just inside the door. A couple of lopsided stools and an old chair completed the furnishings. There was no visible bed, but there may have been another room.

The family shared their bathroom with the team. This consisted of a narrow shed, newly built, presumably in preparation for the team's arrival. It was suspended on a few stout timbers over a long drop. Inside there was a ceramic pedestal with a hole in the bottom from around which flies buzzed busily, there was no plumbing. Users had to take a pail of water into the cramped space with them. From within it was easily possible to peer out between the cracks in the wood. This gave a feeling of exposure and of a total lack of privacy. Candice simply couldn't use it.

Mum worked nights in a factory several miles away and appeared daily just after midday having slept the morning. Dad was a road worker whose day started at 6.00 a.m. so they never saw him during the build days. Together these two jobs covered the cost of food and water for the family, paid back the land loan for the property, and bought their transport to and from work. After that there was very little left. There was a biog of their circumstances back at the site, something the nonprofit did for each family and build team to help with appreciation and understanding for the volunteers.

The children laughed easily. Cesar appeared to have a slight learning difficulty but Candice couldn't be certain. If he did, she feared for his future. This didn't seem a great place to get work if you weren't at the top of your game.

Progress with the build was fast and by the end of the day the shape of the little house was fully formed and the roof panels were ready to go on.

That evening it was the turn of Geoff, one of the nonprofit's senior staffers to speak with the Ablaze group. His brief was to explain appropriate cross cultural mission and how to get the best out of the experience.

He spoke slowly and gently. Phrases that stuck with Candice and resonated for months afterwards had clearly been crafted to distill much information into an economy of words. He may have spoken slowly but his manner and his eloquence indicated a significant intellect:

- *'Most of what you see is not wrong, just different.'*

- *'The Mexican food that you are eating is most likely better than anything the family on your work site will ever eat.'*

- *'Do not laugh at any of their facilities. They are sharing their best with you. Do not add humiliation to their poverty.'*

- *'Some of you have begun to feel hunger probably for the first time in your life. This is a daily experience for your work site family.'*

- *'On camp the bathrooms are basic, you hand carry all the water you use, there is nowhere comfortable to sit, your bedroom is cold. Most of the world lives like this.'*

As the points tacked together in her mind Candice became increasingly aware of the injustice in which she participated daily. She was beginning to be able to articulate the reasons for her lack of personal peace.

Around the camp fire that evening she caught up with Taylor and some of the others. They were all making the best of it. Some were profoundly impacted by what they were involved in, others just getting through the week, longing for the niceties of home. It was amazing though how all of them were quickly adapting after a poor start.

Candice was starting to like some of them. They were less brattish now somehow, it seemed once they got used to the idea, the less they had the more grateful they became. She wondered if there was a macro scale side to this.

Adorable little Cesar and Daniela had nothing, yet they did not exhibit any spoilt tendencies. They were contented, respectful, trying their best to help, retreating immediately when scolded for becoming an obstruction, always anxious to please.

Looking up and down the street the following day Candice continued this train of thought while she got involved in the tricky task of cutting chicken wire which was being stretched over the now tar papered walls of the new house. She observed what she could see of the circumstances of the community as a whole.

Perched on a hillside, with mains water, electricity and some concrete access roads it was a settlement recognized by Mexican officialdom. The views were spectacular but the properties were grim. Being a new settlement pretty much every family was at the same stage of development of their property. Poorly constructed shacks, some two stories high and clearly dangerous were nailed together. Every yard had a home made fence around it, and contained a dog, no wait, a Lord of the Rings style 'warg', with attendant crap everywhere.

She paid particular attention to the Mexican children of the settlement in which the team was working. The children were cruel to animals. They threw stones at dogs. One hefted a big Labrador around with no care whatsoever for which way its joints worked, drawing whimpers and an anguished bark of pain from the animal. This Candice deduced was an educational issue. What would one expect from a culture that taught children at parties to beat a paper donkey until it was destroyed in order to get what you wanted out of it?

The kids played well together. Of course there were disputes, but older and younger looked after one another and responded to one another carefully and respectfully. They had little, but they improvised and innovated. They created and imagined. They laughed and they exchanged little jokes and smiles much of the time.

They have a bunch to teach us about interaction, play and community thought Candice. More words from Geoff's cultural talk last night came back to her:

- *'We come to observe humbly, to learn.'*

Back at camp nobody called Sarah 'Palin' any more. A deep seated respect was setting in for anyone in the distinctive uniform of the trip provider. Sarah was up at 4.30 a.m. with the breakfast crew and was running around camp all day seeing to their group's needs as well as those of the other teams comprising the 1200 or so people currently on the camp site. In the evening time she was serving food, fielding queries, coping with extra requests for items not thought about by Buzz and the remainder of the Amaze team. And she was lovely, truly wonderful.

Candice looked down at her own shapely limbs. She was well aware of the effect her appearance had on others. Girls usually stiffened and found little faults to pick at. Men were either all over her or distinctly awkward in her presence. One flash of a dazzling smile and a hint or two usually got her what she wanted. She realized and was comfortable with the fact that she was by default, and by considerable effort, exceptionally lovely to look at.

Perhaps during this week she was beginning to discover that she could choose to be lovely in the way that Sarah was lovely. The thought appealed to her very much. In fact it left her strangely confused. There were all sorts of cost implications, and when she considered her spiritual growth any steps she had taken in that direction in the past had been quickly retraced whenever there had been an impact on her personal benefits or comforts.

Here it was more possible than usual to reflect on her life because she found her normal context shattered beyond her imaginings. She had been unprepared for how she would feel because she had been unable to visualize in advance what it would be like to lose so many reference points, comforts, privileges and conveniences all at once: washing, eating, drinking, bathroom, seating, working, temperature control, sleeping; all of her normal conditions had been adjusted down. She was aware too that the conditions of the families among whom she was working were lower still, with the added stresses of economic pressure in a shifting and under employing labour market.

There was an anger growing inside her, and something else too. Some imperceptible beckoning, some chink of light in a dark place to which she was inexorably drawn, some scent of water in a desert calling to... calling to what? She was confused, but something was happening deep within her. It was disturbing but it also felt important. Like something suppressed finally getting resolved.

That evening, drawn by a combination of natural curiosity and the incredible noise they were making, Candice, as agreed with Buzz, slipped away to visit the English camp and experience how members of a different culture were coping with their short–term mission trip.

The group, most of whom were sporting a teeshirt or hoodie bearing their logo in hideous puce; were enthusiastically singing worship songs most of which Candice recognized. There was a smattering of Hillsongs in there and bit of Matt Redman, both familiar enough for her to sing along. This despite being unable to see words projected onto the low slung screen at the front, on account of her lack of height, and a significant proportion of the group's tendency to raise their hands when singing.

At first she assumed that all present were into some kind of ecstatic exhibitionist expressive worship style that she'd seen on awful Christian TV shows. She hadn't lingered there, and she wouldn't here if that was *de rigueur* with the group.

However, with the keen eye of a newcomer to a group she quickly discerned three levels of engagement with the worship. There were those carried along with the songs, visibly rapt in their expression of love to God. There were others who were either much more reticent about outward expression, or simply felt they had nothing to express. She was pleased to note that the worship leader was making no effort to coerce involvement from this cohort, preferring to focus on God and let everybody come with her or not as they pleased.

There was for Candice a third far more interesting group, just in front of her, near the back. This was a little knot mainly comprised of lads. Tough rangy looking sporty types of the kind found among the linemen over at the SDSU Athletics Dept. The girls with them were impressed with their bulging muscles and manly devil–may–care demeanours. As expected all members of this group had noticed Candice. She was their kind of distraction. The focus of this subset, once it had stopped gawking was split between the stage at the front, and their own row. One alpha male in particular was doing wonderful impressions of the more ecstatic worshippers. The others in the group were doubled over with mirth, thoroughly enjoying the game and enthusiastically joining in. There was a harassed looking leader nearby who didn't look too pleased, and another older man who glanced at the parody often, wearing a concerned expression. He appeared to be praying.

The music stopped, as did reluctantly the giggling just in front of Candice. Somebody prayed and a youngish speaker, Mark was introduced. He was in his late 20s and athletic looking. Casper would have said he was 'in the ears club' in that they were prominent as was his nose; but he was not unattractive. His voice was strong and his accent so thick he actually sounded like an American comedian trying to do an English accent. Candice was amused.

The talk was something of a testimony and covered a boyhood that had experienced the breakup of his parents' marriage, some wild excesses and a feeling of losing control of life towards the end of high school, particularly regarding alcohol, night clubbing and drugs. It became apparent to Candice that such activities were available earlier in life to English kids. Any of her peers would have had to cross a border for such things, and many did.

Dragged by mum to church, Mark described a sense of pointless attendance at an inaccessible and boring gathering that ran some stuff in other venues for his age group that was slightly more interesting. Overall from his perspective the community lacked the sense of excitement or peer acceptance that clubbing and drinking offered him. He had intended to quit the scene as soon as possible.

At this point the meeting began to take a mildly unnerving turn. The young speaker explained that he had gone along to church one Sunday, bleary from the night before and reluctant as usual. That morning the church had welcomed a visiting speaker. The visitor had started speaking as normal and well into his talk had interrupted himself and pointed at Mark, asking him to get to his feet. Embarrassed and feeling cruelly exposed, even violated, Mark did as he was bidden. The visitor proceeded to pass to Mark publicly a message he claimed to have received from God for all present to hear and to test. He had used a phrase that Mark had found helpful then and still did today. He had said: 'Young man I have received a gift of prophecy. It is the prophet's job to pass on faithfully what he or she is given or shown by God. It is the hearer's job to test what he or she hears.' With that he had gone on to describe with absolute accuracy precisely the most significant issues in Mark's life.

'I just stood there and blubbered,' recounted Mark. 'I felt a total fool regarding this reaction but something had happened to me that I couldn't deny. God had spoken to me, he knew me, he understood me and he wanted relationship with me.'

Mark looked around the tent carefully.

> 'A lot has happened to me and in me since that day. God has asked me to spend a lot of time just alone with him. He's tested me a few times in the matter of what level of obedience to him and his ways I'm prepared to live at.
>
> 'My life, just the way I am has become unrecognizable as a consequence of my journey with God so far. I could not recommend highly enough to you that you begin your own journey of obedience to and relationship with God.
>
> 'I've found over the years that God has begun to speak to me prophetically; and if it's alright with you I'd like to do for some of you what that man did for me those years ago. Is that OK with you?'

Nobody moved everyone was intrigued. Mark went on.

'Now I know a few of you, mainly the ones on the work site with me, but with most of you I don't know who you are and I haven't got a clue about your lives, so just while we've been worshipping together I've asked God about you, because he does know you and I think he has something to say to some of you.'

He pointed to a fellow from the sporty mocking row that had caught Candice's eye earlier. The one who had led the hilarious parody of those engaged in worship.

'Please stand up for me. What's your name mate?'

Slowly, awkwardly the young fellow stood to his feet: 'Karl.'

'Well Karl God wants to say this to you. I don't know if it makes any sense to you but it's about your music. I've not seen you around, certainly not noticed you near the band, but you're a musician right?'

'Well yes I am sort of.'

'Well Karl the issue is this. You think that if you're going to follow God you're going to have to give up your dream of being a rock star. However God says he enjoys it when you play your guitar. He loves to hear you sing. He made you for music. You don't have to choose between God and music, you have to choose between living for him or not. The music will come anyway.'

Karl's face was white, Candice was close enough to notice his legs tremble. His body shook a couple of times as the words rocked him. She could discern immediately that the message was authentic, and something deep inside her leapt at the dynamic she had just seen. Karl sat down. There was a stillness to those sitting around him now; the atmosphere in his row had completely changed.

She had not encountered anything like this before. She'd heard about stuff like it, in fact in the churches she had attended she had been warned to steer clear of fanatics that took what the bible said too seriously, except of course in matters of theoretical theology. The context of her experience of church to date had been neat and tidy: well choreographed worship, glittering pulpits, smart–casual or suited preachers with shiny shoes on plush carpets. If anything she would have expected something like this to be a kind of performance by a middle aged man in a white suit asking for huge amounts of money and pushing people over.

Here though was a youngster in an Adidas track top and jeans, his trainers dragging in Tijuana dust, offering words of hope and life from Heaven itself.

'Massive reevaluation needed,' she thought.

Then Candice heard, almost from a distance words she part feared, part hoped for.

'And the girl behind Karl to his left, yeah the blonde one with the pink jacket. If you wouldn't mind just standing where you are for a moment?'

Candice found herself on her feet. Someone stepped forward and muttered something to Mark.

'I'm hearing you're not from this group. I don't know if it's alright with you, but if you're OK with it I believe God's got something he'd like you to hear.'

Candice shrugged and remained standing, she was incapable of speaking. A mixture of fear, awe, self–consciousness and anticipation washed over her.

'The word I have for you is hungry,' said Mark. 'You're hungry all the time and especially this week you have been hungry in a different way. It's like you've seen something that you're hungry for and God says he's going to satisfy that hunger if you keep pressing on like you have been.'

Mark moved on to others, there were a few more. Every message different, every circumstance described individual.

A final song in which there was 100% engagement in worship from the whole group, and finally an invitation for those that wanted ministry, whatever that was, to come and be prayed with.

Candice found herself sitting with a gentle young woman from a church near London. They prayed together, and as Candice left the big tent venue, tear stained eyes struggling to navigate back to her own camp site in the darkness, legs weak, chest tight from emotion, she felt as if for the first time in her life she had encountered something real of God in the life of the church.

Church! This trip, and in particular this evening, had wrecked her paradigm for what church was. What had happened to her had not been her agenda; she was starting to comprehend that it may have been God's. That the hope she had deep within her was possibly not in vain. She had taken one or two faltering steps towards him, he had come running to meet her.

As she turned in to her blanketed sleeping bag that night Candice had a lot to process, there were many changes to make, and one relationship in particular that had to go.

6.   FOR THIS REASON

Joseph was away for two long years. Throughout that time life in Ibrahim's household settled into a new dynamic. Dina and Eve took charge of the compound, and Eve's older brothers now worked the fields. The women planted three more papaya trees, which grew quickly. They picked and sold mango and papaya, prepared food, took care of the compound, washing clothing and keeping things tidy.

Ibrahim did very little. He drank tea with his friends, slept much of the day under a mango tree on the litter, drank dolo when he could. He was depressed, demotivated and without the drive needed to bring change or hope to his family.

Dina's children played by themselves and with the other children in the street much of the time. There was minimal parental interaction, certainly none with Ibrahim. Life was quiet; the family was in a period of hiatus.

Eve's younger sisters both married church members and joined households nearby. The dowries eased the family's position through the subsequent two food shortages. Eve's brothers were not yet ready to marry. When they did, they were likely to build their own homes within the compound. The family would need more land to support its growing numbers and this was likely to be a problem. Every family needed more land.

Members of some families had drifted away towards the cities, especially those who had attended school. This eased the problems slightly, but there will still hard times ahead.

Eve spent more time around the church now. Florence had taken the role of senior leader focusing her ministry mainly on her organizational and pastoral gifts. A couple of the team, Edward and Samuel had taken on the majority of the church's formal gatherings. Edward and Samuel were both local farmers, one of whom also prepared thatched roof sections which he sold to villagers for their grain stores.

Eve began to visit the sick alongside Florence and learned how to listen and empathize as well as to call on God for his intervention. Sometimes he healed people, many times he did not. Eve learned from Florence to ask more searching questions around sickness than, 'God will you heal this person please?' Questions such as:

— 'What does God want to do through this circumstance?'

— 'What is God calling the church to do in this situation?'

Eve was learning to understand how to work in cooperation with God, from Florence. There was a compassion and empathy which shone in Florence. Her suffering through widowhood and sharing in the multiple tragedies of the human difficulties of her church family had sifted much of the woman that she could have been out of her life.

One day they dropped in for a sad almost non–speaking visit with a woman that had suffered a series of miscarriages and was angry with God over his refusal to bless her womb. Florence listened to her railing against him and later confided with Eve, 'We will never answer these questions. It is foolish to try to explain or resolve issues like these. However I know that God is kind and loving. Bad things happen to people and God is good. These are not two incompatible statements. God will comfort her if she will allow him.'

Eve ate with Florence and her family on Sundays. Florence made sure she always ate fresh fruit, and that the best of any meal was shared with her, as if she were a special guest — even if there was a special guest. Consequently with improved diet Eve's young body strengthened and flowered. Florence observed this with great pleasure and satisfaction. The people in the village were strong. The weak died young and those who survived childhood were of good stock. Eve was a particularly impressive woman, intelligent and tender. Joseph had chosen well.

After lunch Florence took time to teach Eve to read and write, and basic mathematics. 'You will need these skills in the future,' she asserted. Eve was a ready pupil, quick and with a fine memory. She needed to be told something only once, and progressed rapidly. Florence wondered what she could have become if she had been able to attend school. Not for the first time she sighed, glancing down the street at the scores of children, most of whom would never see the inside of a classroom.

When Joseph returned both he and Eve were almost unrecognizable. Both had grown in stature, he in particular had developed in experience and understanding. Two years in and around the capital city had opened his eyes to a world that Eve could never imagine. To explain it, he would have to show it to her.

Eve was concerned that their friendship may have dwindled in the long years of his absence. He would have met many other girls, more educated, more sophisticated, from better families, better looking perhaps.

Joseph had no understanding of such concerns. Yes there had been many other people to meet, impressive, fun, spiritual and beautiful. Such was the way of bible college life and work as an understudy to a nearby church minister. He had been viewed as a novelty and something of a catch by many hopeful young women. However, the regime of the Pentecostal Bible College was a strict one. There was no physical contact permitted between students. Inter–gender relationships were frowned upon before graduation, and if any students were already in relationships before starting the course their ongoing courtship was conducted under strictest supervision.

Old man Oubda, Principal of the college spoke often of the perils of ministry to the men:

> 'Your enemy has been around a lot longer than you. He is more experienced than you and he will take you down if he can.

> 'Money and sex; these two things have robbed the church of its finest talent for as long as I have been on the scene. If you can keep your hands away from the offering and your eyes on your wife, you will have learned two principles that may save your ministry. Money and sex, two of your opponent's most powerful weapons against you young leaders; learn to recognize their power and realize that the moment you drop your guard against them, your ability to function as a Christian leader is in terrible danger.

> 'The church has long taught that you should confess your sins alone in your room, shutting your door pouring out your heart to God. That is a lie. You are to confess your sins to each other so that you can pray for one another and be restored. If you are tempted, tell your friends. No sneaking around now; be accountable to one another.

> 'It has also been my experience that when ministers most need to be accountable, at the time when they are most tried and most tempted; those are the times when they make

themselves least accountable. Do not let this happen to you. Find friends you can trust, and share your journey with them.

'You are fortunate. Back in the Old Testament, when a priest sinned, his restoration would be a very public event. He would have to take a cow and lead it through the camp. You can hear it now, moo... moo! You can imagine the people nudging one another, moo... moo! 'I wonder what old man Oubda has done now!'

Laughter had burbled up from the students.

'For you it will be easy. Confess your sins to one another and pray for one another so that you can be restored. Just do what the book says my boys, do what the book says.'

Joseph had dreamed often of his return to Djigouera and especially his reunion with Eve. Now as he saw her, within minutes of his return to the village: the wonder and delight on his face, the ecstasy of fulfilled dreams in his eyes told her all she needed to know about his faithfulness to the agreement they had made.

They were married in the autumn of that year, just after the harvest.

In deference to the bride's father the celebration had a very traditional feel to it. In all the proceedings took about four days, with family travelling huge distances on the first day, arriving to joyous greetings throughout the day. It was important to be present at a family occasion such as this. However Louis Oudraogo sent his apologies. His travelling days were done, but other family members from Yarbo said that if he continued to look after himself everyone agreed he was good for another ten years yet.

On the second day the women of both families danced while they ground millet using huge wooden pestles in large stone pots. The entire day was spent preparing vast quantities of food. The whole village would be involved in the celebration, and everyone contributed food.

The dowry was presented by the groom's family, two pairs of cows and six goats, a fortune to Florence and an impossible gift without the generosity of the whole church. It was important to Florence to honour Ibrahim and to express a public appreciation of the worth of Eve towards her father.

On the third day, in keeping with tradition Eve was carried by the women of the village from her father's compound to Florence's. This took several hours and whenever a new carrier took over, again in keeping with tradition Eve bawled loudly with sadness that she was leaving her father's family. To do otherwise would have been a terrible insult to him. Eve's heart sang beneath the tears.

There was then a break with tradition as Eve and Joseph made heir vows before God in Church. Steven, Joseph's grandfather, Regional Supervisor for the Pentecostal movement took the service. Florence, resplendent and beautiful looked on with pride and joy as her eldest son married his heart's desire and she gained a daughter of exceptional strength beauty and wit. The sting of pain that accompanied the thought that Philippe could not oversee this day was eclipsed by her joy.

Day four was one of goodbyes and further dancing, and towards the end of the day the community heaved a collective sigh and settled back into normality.

When finally Eve and Joseph's bodies were joined, it was with the ecstatic selfless abandonment of two lovers who have waited for one another. There were no regrets, no feelings of guilt, no furtive fumblings in secrecy and apprehension over the fear of discovery. The community had witnessed and celebrated their love very publicly. Now in the intimacy and privacy of their own space they could begin to construct that most wonderful and blessed gift of the Creator to his children, a marriage.

Eve and Joseph were called to assist Michel Diama, a young and vigorous pastor serving a fast growing church in a strongly Islamic quarter of Ouagadougou, and quickly set about resettling.

A send–off dinner was held in their honour, at which a small but helpful financial gift was made to the young couple.

They walked eight miles to the main road, their few possessions on a hand cart wheeled by Eric. They took the bus, first to Bobo–Dioulasso, staying at Shalom guest house, a place of incredible luxury in their eyes, provided by the churches for Western missionaries. Then they took a much longer bus journey on to Ouaga.

Eve had never travelled by bus before. Fortunately they were on the shady side which allowed her bright eyes to hungrily drink the passing vista as the she sat by the window, without having to draw the thick curtain across. Mile after mile of scrub brush passed her window. Little groups of cylindrical huts with thatched roofs interspaced rectangular shaped block houses such as her father's. Herds of animals drifted between what little patches of pasture were available, watched over by wandering Fulani drovers.

Wonderfully, half way between Bobo–Dioulasso and Ouaga, the bus slowed to allow a herd of elephant to cross the main road. They were in no hurry, walking with measured tread in single file, heading eventually off into the endless bush.

Ouaga was a shock to Eve. The buildings were on a scale beyond her imaginings, despite Joseph's descriptions. Some of the smarter shops had glass fronts, though the majority of the merchants' wares were displayed on hangers or makeshift shelving exposed to the constant dust of the city's traffic. The number of people and vehicles was a bewildering whirl, and everywhere there were compounds, stretching away into the distance in every direction. To Eve the noise was unbelievable. Mopeds sped everywhere many unsilenced, snarling like hornets. The smells and cloying dust that swept into every crevice choked her nostrils and quickly formed an irritating crusting. She noticed that the city folk picked away at their noses routinely in conversation, something that didn't happen in her village, it looked rude to her and although she completely understood why, she couldn't bring herself to do the same.

In the neighbourhood where Michel operated there were very many desperately poor people. He was in the least wealthy *arrondissement* and within that, in an under-developed sector with no piped water. In Joseph's district within the sector there was not a blade of grass anywhere, just the hot reddish dry African earth.

In the dust squatted scores of extremely thin women. Their faces were masked by brightly coloured cloths. They were using pans to sieve the soil into piles of stones, grit and sand. This was their living, and they worked out in the sun from dawn until dusk endlessly accumulating their little heaps of building materials, which they sold for almost nothing. Dirt was cheap.

The little church was built of cement blocks rather than mud, making it a far sturdier structure than the homes that surrounded it. The building was small but the compound very large indeed.

Michel explained that having studied in England at the International Christian Bible College he was fortunate enough to have some support from Italy and Switzerland, firm friends made while in college. Having served his time supporting another church leader in the city, learning the role of pastor, Michel had been sent to lead a team into this very poor district. With his European support he had purchased the compound, and to demonstrate his ownership he had put a wall around it placed on it a very small storage structure.

As soon as they heard that a new church was entering the neighbourhood, a delegation of local Islamic activists had approached the district councilors. They objected strongly to this intrusion. Michel and his little team spent much time in prayer asking for justice. The councilors overruled the objection on the grounds that what Joseph had asked to do, included the provision of adult education and basic health and nutrition advice.

Michel visited his church compound a few days later and on approaching the little structure had found blood smeared on it and a notice: 'If anyone tries to build a church here we will spill blood,' the notice announced, it was anonymous.

Michel had felt a little shiver of fear. He knew that any blood spilled would be that of himself and or his beloved wife Marion.

They prayed a little harder still, decided that the transformation of the community was worth the price of their lives if necessary and pressed ahead with their build. No violence materialized. In time his fears subsided.

The aspect Eve and Joseph enjoyed most about working with Michel was that he had such a range of skills to match a passion for his work. A saxophonist, unusually gifted musically, he built an indigenous worship experience for his congregation which blended Mòoré djembes with Western drums guitars keyboards and brass. It was quite a cacophony at first but with patient coaching, much practice and inspirational leadership it became actually quite heavenly. The Mòoré speaking worshippers swayed and sang. For two hours per week, the desperate, the tried, the unfortunate, the dying and the exploited came together in hope of a better world.

Hope of a better world was not some ethereal after life escapism. Michel was utterly committed to the transformation of his community. His language skills were excellent, and Eve began to add spoken English to her spoken fluent French and first language of Mòoré. She enthusiastically joined Michel's language and mathematics classes held in the compound free to all who would attend.

Michel found some NGOs willing to partner with the church and deliver medical nutrition and hygiene classes. Again Eve picked up some skills. He also passionately believed in micro–enterprise, something World Vision and other Western charities were offering out in the villages.

He persuaded one such body to train him in how to operate a micro–enterprise system with a view to offering it in his community. It depended largely on community leaders. These would oversee the repayment of loans, keeping the honour of the community their uppermost priority. The continuation of loans and financial services would utterly depend upon all members being honourable with money advanced. Micro–finance initiatives normally avoided cities because their populations were too transient. People might take a loan and disappear. Michel was convinced that such a scheme would work in his community. And so it proved.

They named the scheme 'Intègre'. Abdoulaye, a nominal Moslem of standing in the community was entrusted with the ledger. A member of the community known to Abdoulaye and resident locally could open an account with him for as little as 1 CFA. This low start allowed those with insufficient means to open a normal bank account to bank money. Holding cash was a terrible problem especially for the men and there was very little security in the homes, many of the poor had nowhere to keep money.

Eve could testify to what happens to a man with cash in his hand; just the simple ability to be able to bank it made a significant difference to the spending habits of the local people.

It was the loans ledger, however, that brought the most transformation. Very small loans could be advanced for a packet of seeds, or even a basket of bananas for sale at the bus station or in the traffic queues. Repayment could be over a matter of weeks at 5% paid off per week. Interest was set at 8% per loan with a maximum repayment term of six months. All surpluses were used to increase the micro bank's capital, and to pay Abdoulaye a small agreed stipend. Not one person defaulted on a loan, and very soon these hard working people, who had survived with no help for so long, had the tiny assistance needed to get them moving. Goats, bullocks and sheep were bought a few months before the festival of Eid, and sold for a fortune at the time of the ritual sacrifices. Raw materials were fashioned into baskets and simple garments, sold to traders in the markets for a modest profit or direct to travelers and tourists for a substantial profit.

Michel had a saying he came to utter whenever he travelled through the community: 'Fewer people are sieving dirt.' It was true, and it became truer as the months progressed.

Eve's main area of service in church life was visiting the sick and those in need. Here she could quickly discern the difference between those who wanted something and those who needed something. Listening was her greatest strength, and people would be comfortable engaging with her at the deepest levels of interaction. It was here that the voice of God could be heard in her and through her when it came time for her to speak, ministering deep into the souls of the people with wisdom beyond her learning.

She had been taught well by Florence back in Djigouera, but there was something more than training welling up from inside her: an intuitive gifting which naturally flowed into supernatural interaction. There were healings, small matters mainly, a touch from God, authenticating the ministry of the church. And there were deaths. Such was the way of the community. Hygiene was not universally understood, water could easily be contaminated, diet was generally poor and resistance to disease often overcome.

There were no children for Eve for Joseph. It was a concern and one they spoke of often and indeed something which together they enthusiastically made every effort to rectify. The frustration of barrenness did not ruin their love life as could so easily have happened, if anything in the first two years it had the reverse effect.

Joseph had worked well alongside Michel in the two years that he served the little church in Ouagadougou. He had seen tremendous growth and transformation. There were now two services, one in Mòoré and the other which tended to attract a smarter set of congregants, in French. He had worked for Michel according to the advice to graduates of Old Man Oubda at the college always in the back of his mind: 'A man who will not be under authority has none.'

It was however time to move on. He had what he would later describe as a divine restlessness about him. Michel knew it too, and they discussed what to do next.

'It is time for mission' declared Michel to Joseph.

• • •

'When God first called me to this place he gave me vision for more churches. It is time to plant my friend, time to plant. Before we do that I want you to promise me something. Never settle. Leave your way forward open, leave room for God to challenge you, to re-teach you something you thought you knew thoroughly. You will need a vision for the church you're called to serve, God's vision. Vision is not a matter of imagination. It is the product of time spent alone with God combined with the best of your intellect. It is the product of your relationship with him. Unless you have it you will not know the direction you and the people God gives you to lead should travel. Yes my friend, get vision.'

He paused, reflecting for a moment and then made a statement that Joseph would carry for many years: 'Unless you see it before you see it, you will never see it.'

Michel was 32 years old. Joseph had met many men twice his age that could not come close to his effectiveness in ministry or his wisdom. Leaving this place and the godly cover of such a man would cause him to feel exposed and at 23 years old he was maybe painfully young. He was ready to lead though, he knew it.

Michel had friends and relatives down in Bobo-Dioulasso, Burkina Faso's second city approximately 300km to the South West, back in the direction of Djigouera, the place where Joseph and Eve had stayed over when travelling to Ouagadougou. After thought and considerable prayer, he announced a mission trip to an area towards the edge of Bobo–Dioulasso, and called for volunteers to fund their own food and bus fares, travel with him to speak with the people there and proclaim the coming of a Kingdom of righteousness and justice that if they would engage with it, would transform their lives.

There was great enthusiasm among the worshippers; most people had never travelled so far before. Their worship and prayer times took a renewed vigour. Michel found himself looking at the logistics of a large team, thinning it out slightly by restricting members to those who could speak Djula, the *lingua franca* in the area they were to visit. Djula was a derivative of Manding, the root of a cluster of West African tribal languages. It was spoken throughout the Mali border regions so of course Joseph and Eve made the cut.

He had prayerfully thought out a strategy of high risk, but one he most certainly believed was the right course to take.

On arrival in Bobo–Dioulasso the team, 43 strong, stayed in the church building of Michel's friend Serge from the Bible College. He introduced them to Chief Aboubacar who presided over the village of Bandaradougou a few miles to the North. Its people were predominantly Djula with some Fulani and held to extremely traditional values, culture and worship. The village scratched out an existence mixing subsistence farming, producing food for the hungry markets of Bobo and menial work in the city for those with bicycles or mopeds that could make the journey.

Taking care to keep his eyes below the level of those of the Chief, Michel asked if he could tell them the story of the village.

No second invitation was necessary. And the chief was quickly away with his well rehearsed, oft repeated history of the village. Every chief could tell the story of his village, and of course could emphasise when the time came of his own place in the story and the importance of his influence and role.

Michel enquired regarding any prominent fetishes that were used by the chief and his people. Of course the chief was pleased to show Michel his own fetish and described the things he was able to do in commanding the spirits, many of whom he could name.

Michel said he would like to do something extraordinary here, and the Chief, intrigued, invited him to go ahead.

Michel stood by the fetish and raised his voice. 'Bring out your sick, bring out your madmen, I proclaim that the one true Creator God is present to heal and to demonstrate his power!'

The Chief and those villagers who had naturally gathered to watch the large party of visitors were at first taken aback, then an opportunity which the invitation presented occurred to them and they fetched a howling dribbling wild eyed man, chained and emaciated and brought him to Michel.

'This is Sayouba, his mind wanders and he does not understand the ways of ordinary people, he cannot learn. He has been this way since we has very young. He is kept chained because although he is usually docile he sometimes attacks us.'

Michel noted the reaction Sayouba had when he was brought near to him, thrashing, and screaming and drawing attention, and murmured, 'Yes, declare yourselves, my enemies — your time is short.'

Michel looked impassive and called the team to pray and to sing. He spoke directly to Sayouba: 'I command you in the name of Jesus Christ my King, Creator and Commander of the armies of Heaven to release this man.'

Sayouba went very still and appeared for the first time to be quite relaxed. There was no other reaction from him whatsoever.

Michel said, 'Unchain him and give him a little to eat and drink,' which was done.

'We will return tomorrow,' Michel said, 'and then I would like to bring a message of hope to the village. Perhaps, chief Aboubabcar, you can speak first, tell the story of the village again and then I will explain in more detail the ways of the God of Heaven.'

They were back the following day as promised. There was a significant group of people near the fetish. They had needs, and wanted prayer. Sayouba had spoken gently and quietly this morning, for the first time in years. He had spoken of his fears being stilled, of his uncontrollable rage leaving him, and the wonder of peace and quietness in his head.

Everyone who had anything wrong was gathered at the fetish. Michel spoke first to the chief. 'With your permission I would first like you to take down this fetish. Then we will pray for these people since their needs are urgent, and after that you and I will talk with the people.'

'This fetish does not hold the power of your God of Heaven, I will remove it.'

The church in Bandaradougou was born that day, under a baobab tree. People wept as the mercy and healing of the Spirit of God touched their bodies and their souls.

Michel asserted that the actions the chief had taken in allowing him to demonstrate the power of God over the life of Sayouba, removing the fetish, allowing him to speak and permitting the ministry of the mission team to his people in need had shown he was truly a leader who was writing a new chapter in the story of the village. Both he and Joseph preached, speaking of fresh beginnings and of being a new creation, having the opportunity to be brought spiritually alive as God's third self gave birth to life, as Spirit giving birth to spirit.

The baptisms took place in a pool in the nearby river. 38 people were baptized, and the majority of those who came to watch were eager to hear more, wanting to weigh the implications of the seismic shifts taking place in the village's values, traditions and worship.

The spiritual DNA Walter had first brought to old Louis up in Yarbo was faithfully reproduced in the new life introduced by Michel and Joseph in that there was no coercion, simply a demonstration of power accompanied by an explanation of truth. There were some chromosomes within the strands of this DNA which Joseph would come to challenge in the years ahead, but the basic structure was true to the New Testament and therefore highly potent.

Bandaradougou was fortunate in that it was a lush and green area — even in February, weeks after the rains had ended. There would be no more rain now until August at the earliest, but there were good rivers in this district, running from the hills and into the mighty Mouhoun. This river flowed eventually to Ghana and Côte D'Ivoire finding its way to Lake Volta and on to the Atlantic coast. The rivers here would run strongly for most of the year, sometimes reducing to a trickle for a few weeks; becoming dry riverbeds only in years of severe drought.

Michel and his team departed after a few days, leaving Joseph and Eve in the hands of his friend Serge, who provided accommodation and shared his food.

Aboubabcar designated some ground for a church with enough area behind for a compound for Joseph and Eve who had pledged their foreseeable future to this community and to those surrounding it.

The rich red earth and wonderful accessibility of water beneath the ground made the land of Bandaradougou a fertile and viable place for settlement. The people were mainly farmers. Food production was a common occupation found in the Bobo–Dioulasso area, and these villagers had good vegetable growing skills. A few farmed fish by netting off some of the pools in the river. The fish were dried in the sun on racks and spread cloths before being transported, along with vegetables into the city on battered old vans.

These dilapidated vehicles like so many trucks, buses and minibuses had finished their normal working lives in Europe before being loaded with all manner of goods, mainly electrical and driven down to sub–Saharan Africa by daredevil traders.

The trader would sell everything including the vehicle before flying back up to repeat the process. His was a risky business because armed bandits were known to prey on the traders; generally European or South African chancers with good language skills and nerves of steel. Information about safe routes was circulated among these traders although they ran the risk of receiving disinformation intended to reduce the competition, such was the type of men in the mix.

Once they arrived in country, maintenance of the vehicles tended to be shockingly sporadic and focused only upon keeping them running. Wrecks were cannibalized, as were those with terminal mechanical failures, to provide 99% of all parts business, with very few new components being made or shipped. Prices for new vehicle parts were inaccessible, logistics systems were not in place to reliably move such items economically and everywhere the African trading disease of racketeering whenever anybody wanted anything stunted the development of commerce.

Driving skills were picked up along the way, and gaining a driving license was a formality not linked to competence behind the wheel. Consequently road travel was a risky affair, and Joseph was very wary indeed of getting in a vehicle.

Michel left enough money for Joseph to purchase a little moped on which he and Eve travelled to and from Bandaradougou daily while they constructed their little house of mud blocks with assistance from their new friends in the village.

In particular the wiry yet strong Sayouba proved extremely useful. Sayouba had no friends and people were wary of him on account of his lifelong behaviour. His social skills were low and some of the damage done to his relationship with others in the village seemed irreparable. Integration into church life would be an important factor in his new beginning.

Joseph and Eve had to set clear boundaries for him, all the while loving and reassuring him of their commitment to his life. Assisting with the construction of their mud bricks, and then the house itself allowed him to prove to them and anyone observing, that he was capable of working. He was also able to construct basic pieces of furniture, so despite their ability to obtain better elsewhere Joseph and Eve were able to pay him a little and live with his handiwork. They knew that only time would show if anyone else would be willing to pay him for work.

Money was a problem for Joseph and Eve. They had a small level of support from their previous church in Ouaga, but petrol for their travel to and from Bobo was expensive and they needed more income. The new congregation was largely very poor and contributing to funding their church, difficult.

Eve knew how to make baskets and was an excellent trader. She would purchase mangos and papaya in the village and sell them from a tray on her head along with the baskets, with which she festooned her arms. Her pitch was to drivers on the main highway at the points where there were serious traffic delays.

She was young and vigorous, very used to hard work and sustained a punishing daily routine of gathering the women for bible teaching, trading, visiting homes as a pastor; and keeping a welcoming and orderly house. She and Joseph found some positives in their childlessness for this stage of life in terms of their freedom to focus on the development of their property and their church. It remained an issue however and it was clear now that they had a major problem.

Joseph cultivated a little of their land and because their soil was well watered planted papaya trees. These grew quickly, were fruiting in their first year and made a valuable contribution to their income and diet from the second year onwards.

Aboubacar and Joseph held long conversations regarding the future of the village. Of all the pressing needs of the community the need for education for the children was the clearest but there was no obvious way for this to be addressed. They also agreed that basic nutrition and hygiene training were important. Joseph would seek help from the NGO with whom he and Michel had worked in Ouagadougou.

Joseph and Eve discussed the matter of the need for a school later and she and the other women began to pray together about the future of the children of the village. Eve knew the importance of education to their future. The other women had no real concept of prioritizing education over using the children for work from first hand experience but there was a general acceptance throughout the district that education was important. Somehow the people here had a grasp of the accepted facts but had not had the willingness to grapple with it sufficiently to have taken any positive steps forward. The *status quo* of illiterate and innumerate children had remained unaltered and unless deliberate leadership was taken the situation would continue.

The only school that could in any way be described as accessible was five miles away within the outskirts of the city. Eve walked there, assessing the viability of arranging for parents to help each other and share the task of accompanying the children on their journey, thus minimizing the impact on their daily work.

The school was less than welcoming. It was heavily oversubscribed and the charge demanded by the Head Teacher for lessons was prohibitive. In addition to this, the river lay directly in the path of the children on their walk to it. For four months of the year this river would be in flood and the rickety sandbag and plank bridge; used by the villagers to traverse for eight months of the year would be swept away. For the rainy season the only alternative was to walk an additional three miles each way to use the road bridge.

Having assessed the situation she concluded that attendance at the government school was out of the question, they had no alternative but to work towards a more local solution.

Joseph and Eve both had sufficient education to teach others but working their land, trading to earn a living, building the church, initial discipleship training of those recently baptized, and the many others who soon followed them into the Christian community, did not leave adequate time for launching a school.

As the women met with Eve to pray earnestly for a teacher to come, Joseph and Aboubacar agreed that the church should take responsibility for some land that would be set aside for a school if in the future they could find a way of building one. The land allocated was close beside the church and Joseph immediately planted the plot with a grove of eucalyptus trees to prevent any other building being placed there.

The trees would grow into a valuable crop and discourage biting insects, a constant problem to the villagers which brought disease and death to small children in particular.

Church meetings continued to take place under the village's prominent Baobab tree. In the meantime Serge, the pastor from Bobo, introduced Joseph to Issa, a friend who represented Temples Ministries, a nonprofit based in the USA committed to collaborative church building. Most of their activity was in Mali but they were expending the operation into Burkina Faso.

Issa proved to be a wonderful supporter. If Joseph could commit to building the block work and internal fabric of a church, Temples Ministries would design, build and ship them a steel frame for the construction.

Joseph spoke with the congregation, explaining the advantages of having a building, especially in the rainy season. There was a general commitment among this group of mostly very poor people to provide what they could towards the cost of cement and moulds for the bricks and the corrugated iron for the roof. There was an expert builder in Serge's congregation prepared to give some time to supervising the construction if the villagers could host and feed him for a few weeks.

Michel's church sent a substantial gift having asked their friends in Switzerland for help. He delivered the gift in person visiting them rather self–consciously in a beautiful 10 year old Nissan Patrol 4x4, a gift from his European friends.

With funds in hand and the tremendously enthusiastic will of a village catapulted into life by a shared project, the community raised their crudely constructed but structurally sound church with their bare hands within six months of their first meeting beneath the Baobab tree.

When the rains came, the new congregation at Bandaradougou had a building fitted out with benches, a raised platform for the speaker at one end complete with a roughly constructed pulpit stand for notes and bibles. There were shuttered windows but there was no door, just a frame. Funds had run out before they could purchase one and it was seen as unnecessary at this stage. Such a luxury would have to wait. Many of the villagers' homes had no doors; they made do with just a rough piece of cloth and dog on guard. Why should the church not do the same?

Michel came himself to lead the first meeting in the new building. He brought his saxophone. Issa from Temples Ministries brought his camera, everyone gathered outside to smile, and the good folks from Temples over in Oklahoma had another picture on their office wall. They may have gained some satisfaction at seeing their African friends gathered in front of a decent sized fairly nondescript hall with no glass in the windows, no architectural decoration except a wooden cross up above the pitched roof, and no door. They could not in their wildest dreams have understood what it meant to Joseph and Eve. In their eyes the building was massive, and although at that time they could all gather at one end and it seemed a bit outsized, explosive growth was now possible without further construction.

Michel spent a few days with Eve and Joseph. It was a time filled with joy and swapping stories, some of them very sad, most filled with the hope and progress so typical of life in Michel's church. The young couple gave all thanks and glory to God for what had happened in this place. They were deeply appreciative of Michel for his ability to hear God and run with a strategic mission and for recognizing them as capable young leaders and handing the initiative to them.

Michel was extremely encouraged himself, noting that the time of any dependency this plant had on the mother church would soon come to an end.

He and Joseph had participated in something that Walter had noticed eighty years previously. It was no accident that God had directed his team to the Mossi people. Once they caught discipleship as a lifestyle, they planted churches that planted churches, quickly proliferating the impact of the gospel of Jesus Christ throughout the region of Francophone West Africa.

On the return journey just as he came into the outskirts of the city, exhausted from the long journey Michel Diama fell asleep at the wheel of his car. He smashed into the front of a house and died of his injuries at the scene.

7.   LEAVING

Candice stood sobbing as the Mexican pastor, a gigantic man by the name of Jorge–Luiz with an impressive moustache, prayed for the little Mexican family whose house they had built.

She had experienced a wetness around the eyes when Courtney, one of the young people whom Buzz especially favoured, had handed the key to Pablo. However when Pablo attempted to thank the team for the house on behalf of his family, things got a little emotionally out of hand.

'I never dreamed I would one day have a house in which to raise my family. I have nothing I can give you to…' His voice tailed off to nothing as his mouth dissolved into wavy lines of helplessness and shame.

Candice howled. Seeing up close the indignity of receiving help in the context of real and desperate need was too much. She felt for this hard working humble decent man. He had done nothing to deserve being under–employed, going largely unrewarded for giving of his best. Under–educated by a system that had failed him, exploited by globalization, and carrying the same hopes and dreams as every other husband and father, he had done his best — and his best was in need of help.

Candice recalled the guidelines she had heard in the briefing she had received from Geoff in his session on crossing culture. It made a little more sense now. She flinched at the thought of what her team of teenagers might have done to Pablo and Gabriella without it.

> 'They may not look very grateful, the speed with which the house goes up, and having a big team of you running around on their land may place the family in shock. You might overwhelm their ability to cope with change. They will probably not be at their best.
>
> 'Respect their dignity. Honour them for the privilege they have given you of helping in their need.'

Geoff was a smart guy. Doing this kind of humanitarian work without that kind of guidance might have done severe damage.

After the handover of the keys, there was a little street party for friends and relatives. The team had made extra tortilla wraps and brought additional juice to share with those who came.

Candice was pretty sure that this day would stay etched in her mind until her grave. Something had truly broken in her. She now owned a measure of brokenness that working for this little family had given her. It would be the key that unlocked her future.

That evening, their last night in camp, the team thanked La Cocina for their wonderful food. 'Being truly hungry every day has affected their attitude to gratitude,' said Buzz, which rather memorably if irritatingly summed the situation up for Candice. Knowing that despite not eating what they would have preferred, they had still eaten better than the local Mexicans had also impacted everyone at a profound level.

Candice asked Buzz why the group was not following the guidelines the trip provider had given them regarding debriefing.

'Oh I don't usually bother with all that,' he responded, 'it's all a bit navel gazing to my mind, we can do without it.'

Candice was concerned: 'We were warned that unless the kids get to think through what has happened on the trip and practice expressing those thoughts, then many of the things they've learnt could be lost. They also point out that it is useful to be prepared with some well considered thoughts, to help explain their experiences to the fund–raisers and to the church. No–one is going to offer support in future if the kids can't report back why this trip was important to them. It's supposed to be part of respecting the older generations that have invested in it. Everything else they briefed us on has turned out to be good advice, why would they be wrong about this?'

'It's not wrong, just different,' quipped Buzz, smartly closing the subject for further debate. He didn't have time for this. The day had been an emotionally tough one; he was physically exhausted after a week of working 24–7. It was not the moment for a discussion on a radical alteration of his priorities and scheduling. Candice was not as good a wordsmith as Buzz and had not lost this mild disagreement because he was right and she was wrong. She just didn't have the tools to overcome the combination of his talent and his ego.

The trip provider had managed to source solvents to clean the vans, and Buzz insisted this was done before they were loaded, a very wise move as all the kids were keen to get going and this extracted maximum effort from them. Not everything he did was annoying, thought Candice.

The trip back up to the border was even more meaningful to the team than the journey South, just a few days earlier. Now that they had spent some time in one of the official settlements, they could understand the culture more thoroughly.

As the dusty boulder strewn hillsides passed before their eyes they could see unofficial settlements up in the more inaccessible canyons and the higher parts of the slopes furthest from the roads and shops. Checkerboard looking newer estates of neat square almost Middle Eastern style houses stretched for miles along the valleys. Row after row, every house unimaginatively identical, all arranged in neat blocks were laid out beneath their highway. Blair, a fount of knowledge on all things Mexican had explained that these were the habitations of the slowly emerging middle class. They had mains drainage, electricity and some estates had internet. Their owners were managers and supervisors, more professional types who had gained an education or an edge. The team was viewing Tijuana success in all its ordinariness.

Crossing the border from Mexico into the United States was a far more laborious and time consuming process than the reverse. Very long lines of vehicles ground slowly towards the barriers. Traders plying Mexico flags, hats, snacks and candies worked the queues. Churros, long cactus shaped cinnamon donuts covered in sugar, proved very popular in the vans at one dollar per bag. Candice observed sugar sprinkling everywhere and mentally reserved another half hour for sweeping out the vehicles later.

Homeland security wanted an individual conversation with every person crossing the border. This took a very long time and necessitated everyone exiting the vehicles, taking their luggage through the lines waiting patiently for the pleasure of speaking with an unsmiling humourless armed officer. Sniffer dogs walked the lines nosing curiously at bags. Candice could understand something of the indignity Mexicans expressed when comparing arrangements at the Canadian border to this orderly nightmare, a daily ritual for many workers operating in the 'free zone'.

Tearful goodbyes were made between exhausted young people and leaders. Buzz was everywhere, high fiving and exchanging a particularly irritating 'whoop whoop!' which had randomly become a craze on the trip with the kids. Relieved parents anxiously scanned for their progeny, bags were trailed into SUVs and families roared away towards favourite food outlets.

• • •

Casper headed down towards the church in response to Candice's call, once the vans were cleaned and the drivers had departed to drop them off at the rental company. They were all on damage waivers so there was no stress about any little dents or bits of fixture or fitting that had succumbed to the stresses of teenage mission team transportation.

The Lexus, minus its previously sported appendage, nosed into a space in the parking lot. Candice's bags were wedged into the limited stowage space in the car, and he whisked her away with the top down.

'Where would you like to go? Shall we grab something to eat?'

'First, a long power shower, then the Blue wave, then bed to sleep for a month.'

The apartment in point Loma was incredible after the privations of mission life in Tijuana. Every item of furniture ensconced the user in luxurious comfort. The fittings were perfect; everything was plated in gold or made of marble or granite. Uplighters and downlighters operated on dimmer switches and presence detectors automatically activated lights and fans in the bathroom. Crockery and cutlery, household appliances, rugs, cushions, curtains, blinds all were dazzlingly beautiful and made to the highest quality. On the walls flat porcelain friezes and lovely original watercolours restfully contributed to the ambience and all the colours balanced wonderfully. Old man Scales certainly lived well, especially as this was his second home, and he had been away from base for almost half of his service life anyway.

Candice allowed her mind to run over the little shack which had been home to Pablo, Gabriella, Daniella and Cesar. She recalled her first glimpse of the numbing squalor that had greeted her enquiring gaze when she had first entered. She looked up at Casper's ornate gilded ceiling with its carved wooden rotating fans and gorgeous gilded lights. She thought of the sheet of polythene slung from the four corners of their ceiling to keep the drips off the busted sofa. She shuddered recalling the stench of the place, the consequence of no plumbing and that of unrefrigerated food and un–wiped surfaces.

She was overwhelmed by the scale of the difference, and as the water cascaded over her body in the shower, rather than luxuriating in the wonderful cleansing, she sobbed and moaned in the privacy of the space.

Showered and hungry she headed out to Blue Wave with Casper. It was over fish tacos that she steeled herself and began the conversation which could wait no longer.

'Casper we need to talk.'

'Sure honey, tell me all about it.'

'I can't do this any more.'

'Can't do what honey?'

'I can't spend my life on what is destroying my soul. I love everything about our lifestyle. I adore you and think you're amazing. I'm thrilled to be a cheerleader and love to do my thing at the games. I have my bachelor's and I'm excited to be finally looking for a job in sports science, it's what I've worked towards. I love it all. It's just that deep inside of me I know most of it is not what I want my life to be about.'

Casper put down his fork. He was on that list she'd just run through and this was sounding serious.

'What's going on? Has something happened to you?'

'Yes I have become a disciple of Christ.'

'What? You're already a Christian, you've done a discipleship course, what are you talking about?'

'Down in Tijuana I figured out that Christian discipleship is not a course and becoming a Christian is not a transaction. I see that more clearly now and some of what I'm seeing now simply wasn't visible to me before. Casper I can't tell you what this trip has done for me. I have come alive like never before and I see the world differently. I have this appreciation of God and what he's about in the world that I'd never noticed. It's like it's all hidden in plain view, and once you've seen it, you can't ignore it.'

Casper felt uneasy but didn't panic. He had not expected this, and right now his priority for interaction with Candice was a romp together. He had missed her and was somewhat inflamed by a surprisingly faithful abstinence partly facilitated by a wonderful week of bachelor activities with Chip. These had included sailing his dad's Sunseeker, a day on the golf course, an evening watching the Padres get crushed by the Jets, the movie theatre for a touch of gore and two days at sea sport fishing. It had not included women.

'I need to get some space to clear my head and work out what I want to do. I want to move back to my mom's.'

'Now wait a minute sugar, what happened to all that "boom bring it on baby?" Are you saying you need space from me, lover–girl?'

'Yes I am, and I know it seems a bit sudden but, well thinking about us, we don't really talk do we? I mean I don't think I know you at all. I have no idea what's going on in your head, what you really are inside behind all the action man stuff. You're like this impossible dream man to me, I just don't know if I mean that much to you. Sure there's lots of fun and stuff. In fact I can't remember a time when I've had more fun than since I got with you. You're a beautiful man, really; the fulfillment of everything I ever wanted. You are — were — my dream. It's just that I don't think I was clear enough on what I really wanted, kind of not dreaming straight.'

Now he did panic. Like a spoilt child unable to comprehend losing out on candy, the awful reality that he wasn't going to get any action from her tonight, and that she might actually want out of the relationship, began to look probable.

Part of his psyche, the mean self–centred part, that wasn't always totally manageable cut in at this point. Here was a chance to be free of her, to cut and run, play the field again. He would do what the cheerleading team would do in due course; get another blonde. What was unthinkable was that *she* might dump *him*. That would be just too humiliating. Nobody dumped Casper Scales.

'Well you were quick enough to get this thing on girl. You need to make up your mind. You telling me if it's all off? Because nobody messes me around, not you Sugar, not nobody, OK? If you want to go running back to momma, good luck to you. Let me know if I fit in to your plans when you've had your bit of space and I'll see if I'm still interested.'

She blanched at his tone, realizing that a conversation now was not going to be a rational one.

'I'm sorry Cas, I'll get my things.'

She made a call to her mom and she was gone. He didn't even help her load the elevator or her Jeep, just sat silently watching baseball.

He sat in the apartment trying to comprehend what had happened. On one hand he had a solution to a particularly difficult situation and was free of someone who at one level had the possibility of becoming a pain. On the other he was extremely disappointed to be alone tonight. He headed off down to the sea front boardwalk with a dangerous determination to hit a bar.

Candice hugged her mom and burst into tears. She was emotionally exhausted, bewildered and confused by how her return to civilization as she had known it, had gone. The unspoken exchange between the two women told her mom all she needed to know at this stage about the relationship crisis.

Candice went to bed mumbling something about laundry. Her mom dug around in her bags and stood staring in disbelief at the mud and cement encrusted garments that were clearly too much for her washer dryer's capacity.

'Three loads here,' she muttered, busying herself with the task. 'Typical! Leaves at a moment's notice, comes back when she needs some washing done! Still acts like a student!' Her mind typically fondly judgmental, she was pleased to have her daughter home, if slightly disappointed that such a fine prospect as Casper hadn't worked out.

Garry arranged a feedback session for the mission trip kids in the Sunday service. As with all services the programme was timed, and the team was given 11 minutes, a generous allowance given that there was a baby to dedicate and a special focus on the forthcoming programme of seeker services to get through.

Buzz hadn't devoted too much time to arranging the session. He also had a lot to fit in so rather artistically and on the principle that a video paints a million words he had his people talk at the mics while the video they'd made of the trip played silently on the big screen in the background. Very unfortunately, the version shown was the unedited one, a consequence of poor file naming, and failing to run a full test prior to the service.

The congregation was therefore treated to an opening scene with Buzz silently speaking through the open window of a van on which was emblazoned the word 'PENIS' with attendant arrow towards his head. Most people found it very hard to decide what to do with their faces at this hilariously ironic moment but there was plenty of shocked merriment in most eyes.

Three individuals from the team were given two minutes each, with Buzz topping and tailing. Naturally, those stepping to the mics were the ones most eager to do so.

Taylor went first. Her testimony centred around the fun they'd had in the vans, working the showers, trying to make the best of rank food and how much she'd enjoyed being in the team.

Courtney simpered and mentioned how cold it had been at night and how she'd had to put up with her sister's snoring. She said it was good building the house together but she gave no detail about what the construction process had been or what she had learned.

Jon told everyone what an excellent trip it had been using words like 'wow', 'incredible', 'cool' and 'brilliant'. What was incredible and brilliant was not described. He ended his ramble with a 'whoop whoop' which was enthusiastically returned by other trip members.

At the wrap up Buzz was feeling very angry about that opening scene on the video. He gathered as much graciousness as possible, thanked everyone that had helped out at the fund-raising events and thanked the parents for trusting him with their kids. He failed to mention the Mexican family at all.

The only lasting memory the congregation had of the presentation was a particularly excruciating label of Buzz.

• • •

After the service, over excellent coffee and cookies in the church café, Candice approached Ellen, Garry's impossibly beautiful wife. Candice's approach was with a view to following up on her determination to make deliberate changes in her own spiritual development, and to be accountable to someone for it.

Would Ellen agree to help her in her discipleship process? Ellen didn't have a clue what Candice was talking about.

'You've done a discipleship course surely?'

'Well yes, I did that when I went for baptism.'

'I'm happy to meet up with you, talk about where you're at; maybe gather some other 18–25s and do some bible study.'

'That might be neat, but I was thinking more about being stretched, developing in spiritual gifts, addressing areas of sin I'm struggling with, that kind of thing. I've been reading a book on working with the poor and the author talks a lot about discipleship being a fire that is caught not a theory that is taught.'

Things were moving quickly away from Ellen's comfort zone. She had become a church leader more by default than choice. She had been a gorgeous girl with no shortage of offers when Garry had swept her off her feet. Their love had quickly blossomed into a permanent relationship.

She had worked at Raytheon where she did some data analysis on stats for the radar guidance testing schedules, a great job gained straight after college where she'd studied statistics and math. She hadn't really thought of one day becoming one half of a senior church leadership marriage and where there were all kinds of expectations placed upon her.

In all honesty, she hated the way people spoke of and to her husband when he wouldn't pander to their expectations and demands. She had watched his dreams of changing the world down size to surviving local church politics and building a system that would be an effective Christian outpost in a rapidly disengaging culture. Her role was fast becoming an inescapable prison in which her clothing, manners, hosting ability, speech, reading material, knowledge of theology and ability to run fund-raising events were all the subject of endless scrutiny, criticism and punditry from women married or hoping to be married to men of less prominence in the church than Garry.

Frankly she had no desire to get into any kind of close relationship with anyone from the church. She was going through a process of withdrawal from this community, increasingly seeking escape from the suffocation of 'public' life among a private club. Of course she had nobody for herself in the role that Candice was requesting; she was as alone in leadership as Garry.

Ellen was a smart girl. She kept her unruffled caring expression in place, thought on her feet and steered Candice towards a woman in her early fifties called Pamela Harris. Pamela was home from having served as a missionary in South Asia for over twenty years. Her kids were going through college education so she and her husband had decided to prefer their own children over their mission activities for this crucial period of time and were taking an extended US posting with their organization.

Ellen had chosen well. Candice had found someone who could help her, and she quickly began to grow and develop in her relationship with God as the extraordinary Pamela opened her eyes on a window to life beyond California and Tijuana, into Asia's teeming millions and the suffering of countless women and children perpetuated every day by injustice and poverty in some of the countries where she had worked.

Candice started to experience a longing to throw in her all with the poor and the needy of Asia. She began to devour information, particularly relating to South East Asia. Places like Laos, which she discovered had been the victim of carpet-bombing at the hands of the United States during the Vietnam War. Apparently, more tons of high explosive per square mile had been dropped on Laos than any other country in the history of the planet. She began to understand the impact of the behaviour of what were understood to be Christian countries by other cultures whose worship and traditions were completely different to those with a strong Judeo–Christian influence. In Laos for example, to be a Christian was to be an enemy of the state. This matter related directly to the behaviour of what were seen to be Christians, supporting anti–government factions and carpet-bombing women and children.

Pamela was a lifelong missionary, whose personal experience of exposure to the threat of violence, hunger, disease and imprisonment had shaped her character. Her husband Rick was the son of missionaries, someone uniquely positioned to understand Asia from the viewpoint of a national, and the US from the viewpoint of a remote citizen who had completed his college education and seminary here.

Candice became a regular visitor to their home, and found in Rick, for the first time in her life, a man who was absolutely immune to her beauty. There were things far important to Rick than looking at women. He'd nailed that sucker years back. Working for a while in Thailand where the pros grab you on the street, even when you're walking with your wife, had caused him to face his sexuality and master it.

In response to the question, 'How do you cope ministering in an environment which is rife with sexual opportunity and where an American man is a constant target for seduction?' he would reply simply, 'Abhorrence.'

• • •

Casper was having no such success with keeping his pants on. He had been through a series of girlfriends since his Facebook page re–flagged to 'single.' In fact it was only when he came to amend it that he realized it had stated 'in a civil partnership' since Chip had come down to stay. 'I may just have to kill him,' he thought smiling broadly.

Casper was just beginning to realize what he'd lost. None of the girls he dated could hold a candle to Candice gymnastically, aesthetically and more important actually, personably. He decided to take her out and see where she was at. Maybe he could salvage something.

The evening had been very awkward indeed. Frankly, he had missed her and wanted to win her back. That gave the date a frisson of emotional edge he'd not felt for some time. She had told him the night she left that he didn't really share his dreams with her, so tonight he gave it his best shot. He actually enjoyed his own monologue very much. He quite impressed himself, continuing and furthering a long love affair.

She had listened impassively to a long list of achievements as he warmed to the task of impressing her.

Droneview product development had continued rapidly. Marcus had perfected a gyro stabilization which when combined with a really neat software intervention had meant that live and recorded camera feeds were in crystal clear HD. All camera shake had been virtually eliminated, and auto–focusing constantly updated however erratic were the manoeuvres the craft was directed to perform. He had registered patents linking drones, gyroscopic stabilization, and the software governing them. He had the patent for any drone with shake compensation software going forward, substantially increasing the worth of the company.

He had found a buyer for Droneview Realty Inc. and Skycam its subsidiary, complete with the existing contract to Fry's. He had persuaded the buyer to take Chip as managing Director going forward with a significant shareholding.

Marcus he took with him into CaMPuS Innovations, a neat little play on their initials and the chemical symbol for gold. The name also carried a link to his desire to make the most of the invitations he was getting from young tech hopefuls to bring projects born in the universities and colleges of the US to market.

The proceeds from the sale of Droneview were so significant that all three friends were set up for many years to come. Even after laying down considerable security for the future Casper was at liberty to place large amounts of liquid capital into high risk ventures.

Casper's plan was a clearly thought through if well trod path; he was not without friends at the cutting edge of commercial theory and practice and the guidance he'd received from them was very sharp indeed. Marcus, along with any top rated emerging talent he cared to recruit, would bring expert assessment and innovative ideas to design projects that appeared to have merit. Casper with his track record of driving success was a point of connection between the startup and strategic contacts in the commercial world.

His was also a face that angel funders could trust. These high rollers bought in at the crucial phase between design and the gaining through shareholding investors of the capitalization needed to take a new technology company to floatation. If, immediately before or after floatation, one of the really big commercial players came in and bought a company of his 'off the peg' then those heavily invested at the angel stage would cash in their chips and toast their boy; investors at the capitalization stage would reap exceptional rewards too.

Casper told Candice he was convinced he had the wit and drive to make things happen; that much he had proven already but he felt there was far more in him than had been seen so far. He knew intuitively what he wanted to do, and having identified an opportunity could exploit it with style, carrying in his mind clarity regarding what he wanted to make and keeping aware of the emerging markets and the media opportunities to exploit. He was young and exciting, thus his blue chip graying contacts were as keen to tap into his vigour as were Marcus's pimpled peers hungry for a route to launch their ideas.

Candice did her best to follow his outpouring of dynamic energetic enthusiasm. She was excited for him and really did care about his dreams. However in the weeks since the mission trip her reprise of what she was about had caused a sea change in her life's priorities.

She hit Casper with a searching question: 'What are the values that you're working to?'

Easy, he thought, the answer was obvious. He had mission and values statements all over the place back at his shiny new office downtown, and he'd alluded to them often enough even tonight. Most of his core staff team could recite them: 'We operate to the highest quality assurance standards, we seek to cultivate an atmosphere of creative excellence, seeking always to delight our customers with design innovation and style, and to provide our stakeholders with the highest yields on their investments.'

Candice was slightly exasperated: 'No Casper, those are the values of the company, I meant your values.'

'Mine? Well I guess I want to continually achieve and constantly upwardly review my personal goals by maximizing my strengths. I want to build a great team of exciting people each with the resources, continuous education and encouragement to reach their potential. I want to look after everyone who's with me by creating a great standard of living for me and my friends; and I want to do something exciting with every year of my life.'

Touching Smyrna

Candice was constantly amazed by this focused, driven, excellent man. On one level he really was a dreamboat, but on another she'd barely even started on him yet and was certainly not impressed by what she'd heard there.

'Making a shed load of money features heavily in there?'

'Of course it does. That's the reason I am in business.'

'And when you talk about the team who's with you are you including the workers in your factories who build product to high standards for chicken feed; because in their despair they and their kids will take a job, any job to keep from destitution. Are you making sure that you are not taking advantage of the desperate decisions of poverty; like selling bodies or children? Does it matter to you that the jobs offered are almost without employment rights and pay wages that perpetuate poverty?'

Casper was slightly taken aback, even affronted by this salvo from a sports science specialist with no commercial education and whose chief achievement in life so far was being thrown up in the air in front of 70 000 people all intent on watching something else.

The timing of the challenge however was amazing. He found himself wondering if there was some kind of divine subterfuge going on. He'd met with a business analysis team only that week whose presentation was still etched in his mind and resonated with Candice's words. The team had encouraged him to look beyond China for future manufacturing solutions. The current data was showing that the Philippines might be a good strategic move. Here there was the highest education to poverty matrix; statistics enabling procurement of competent employees for low wages for the medium to long term future.

The country enjoyed a good political relationship with the USA, despite the behaviour of the Pacific Fleet in port over the last half of the 20th century and the rise of Islamic extremism in the Southern Islands. The hot advice was that with a growing middle class in China, manufacturing costs would rise there as quickly they had in Korea, where real estate was now as expensive as in Japan.

There apparently were also good ratios of education to poverty developing in Bangladesh and Pakistan, though in both countries electricity supply was fragile. They were also affected currently by political unrest and despite huge aid payments, significant anti–American sentiment. This may change of course and there were always intermediaries through whom business could be conducted.

What chimed with Candice's question was the importance of the education to poverty matrices which had been a large part of the presentation he'd enjoyed. For successful low–cost production there needed to be a significant number of people with education but few prospects, and a large pool of work hungry peasants. He had not for one moment considered their stake in his projects. In fact if he was honest he was most interested in keeping their *status quo* as unchanged as possible.

'The truth is Candice, I cannot fix those problems, and no, I do not consider the workers in the production lines to be stakeholders nor team members. They are for my purposes merely a component in the machine of industry.'

'So it's all about the numbers, rather than the people right? Is that because they're not Americans and they didn't go to Dartmouth?'

Candice moved on, Casper kind of wished she wouldn't.

'And God, where does God feature in your personal list of core values?'

'I seek to conduct my business honestly and as a good Christian. I pay my taxes — boy, do I pay my taxes! — and it looks like I'll be funding a whole load of healthcare and God bless America,' quipped Casper evasively.

'What did you mean when you gave your life to Christ and got baptized?'

'It meant that I'd accepted Christ as my Saviour and Lord and that I would seek to live for him as best I can.' He knew the answers of course. In fact he'd explained as much many times to youngsters from the projects during football mission outreach programmes. Now Casper was feeling very uncomfortable indeed. These words of his had a kind of hollow ring. A high minded set of ideals that he'd signed up to as a teenager that had got overwritten a bit in the years since. It was time to turn the tables.

'OK Candice, let's not make all this about me, tell me your values. Don't forget the bit about taking a ride on an Ivy League college football player's career by shaking your ass and moving in with him at the drop of a hat.'

Candice blushed at the cheap shot. She was well thought through on this issue though. She had wrestled with little else for weeks.

'And moving straight back out when she got a hold of her senses.' She couldn't resist that. 'I am trying to find out what matters to God, beginning with the not incidental fact that I matter to him; and reshaping my priorities so those things matter to me.'

'Is that it?' Casper was impressed with the succinct summary, and kind of wished he'd got some spiritual and moral rectitude into his own but hers seemed a bit short on goals and outcomes. He wanted a bit of flesh on these neat little bones.

> *'Well there is a bit more detail involved in how it all lands. My values centre on the fact that I have chosen to become a disciple of Christ. For that reason I have humbled myself before God and I'm trying to utterly turn my back on a mindset that had me making a self-seeking attempt to claw my way into the security the systems of this world have to offer me.*

'I know that there are two things — fruits the bible calls them — required of my life, that matter to God. These are things which I can produce by cooperation with him. Despite a prayer life until recently arranged around what I wanted from God, I am learning to want what God wants, rather than what God's got.

'Here are the two things I believe he wants from me, and indeed from every human being.

'Justice: that is, have I acted justly and have I done all within my power to speak truth into injustice seeking to influence those with temporary power invested in them by God to have regard for those with none?

'Righteousness: that is, active goodness. Have I been behaving in the way that God would in my interaction with others? It includes putting right the damage done to others by injustice or unrighteousness; such as serving the unfortunate, binding up wounds, doing right by people in need and so forth.'

'We're not going to find each other are we?' Casper was stating the obvious. There was a gulf between them. The evening was going nowhere, she was making him feel nervous, and he had about as much chance of getting her into bed later as he had of being pecked by a dodo; time to cut and run.

'Candice you're sounding like a fanatic.'

'Casper why does committing to spiritually positive values make me a fanatic; and you get the right to call me one from your lofty position of commitment to shallow self-serving crap? Of course I'm impressed with what you do and how you do it, my problem is with the why.'

They left, both confused: she, because she longed to convince this wonderful man that authentic Christian discipleship would bring him from death to life; he, because Candice post-mission had forced him into an uncomfortable re-evaluation both of her and himself. She had morphed from being an object predominantly for eye candy and bedroom entertainment to a force to be reckoned with, a far more attractive proposition for relationship.

As he re–ran the conversation later he had a clear choice to make. He could allow this feisty little gorgeous disciple of Christ to radically reshape his life, and perhaps he might win her heart and save himself in the process; or he could dismiss her as a fanatic and move on.

He moved on. He was too invested in his investments.

• • •

The Ablaze mission planning team met two months later to discuss the mission schedule for the next three years. Buzz was enthusiastic about heading back to Mexico for more building trips. He met with resistance from Taylor's mom. There were concerns about the way the catering had been handled. Some of the kids had complained that they had gotten hungry and that there was not enough food to sustain the team through the day.

Buzz was quick to point out that there was plenty of food, and that it was excellent, it just wasn't pizza, donuts and hamburgers, consequently kids that were used to stuffing themselves had eaten more sensibly and experienced normal healthy hunger cycles.

Taylor's mum Trixie, an impossibly well turned out forty something that, along with her very cool husband did something important in TV production up in LA. She and Blake lived in La Jolla at the weekends. They were big supporters of the church missions, hence her presence at the planning meeting. She was offended by the unmade inference that she fed her kid pizza, donuts and burgers. She did of course, but didn't like to be seen to do so. She didn't say anything but he had lost her. She would oppose anything he suggested.

He pointed out that there had been excellent spiritual, physical, social and educational outcomes for most trip participants.

Casper wanted to know what the spiritual outcomes were. Buzz found it hard to give any hard evidence of spiritual growth that would not otherwise have been seen. Casper pressed Buzz about any controversial or extreme doctrinal stuff that had been covered. Buzz couldn't think of any, but pressed for a bit more clarity on what Casper meant. Casper stated that without wanting to name names or disclose sources he'd come across some evidence of team members becoming somewhat fanatical.

He was still smarting from his breakup with Candice, and blamed the mission trip for wrecking her normal healthy church membership and turning her into some kind of suffragette. He was angry at what Buzz had done and would oppose anything he proposed.

Garry saw something advantageous in bringing change to their current short term mission partner. He could avoid that conversation he had pending; regarding how they could do their thing more stylishly and not much less authentically. He wasn't sure they would go with him on that. It might be far easier to cut and run to another provider closer to his approach.

He called a vote on youth mission trip options for the following year, and to his absolute consternation Buzz found his Tijuana trip cancelled in favour of him being required to set up something a bit closer to home, with a new and more adventurous trip maybe to Africa or somewhere the year after that. 'Closer to home?' he thought, 'Tijuana's just the other side of the wall!'

Buzz resigned as youth leader two months later, taking a post with the Harvest Community over on University Heights. The reason he told his friends was that he didn't appreciate decisions being taken over his head.

Actually the little job satisfaction he had gotten and the most spiritual headway he had made with the kids over the last couple of years had been linked to the mission trip. He was mortified that the church hadn't valued the contribution the trip had made to his work (and therefore to their strategy for developing kids) more than it had. There was no exit interview in which his deeper reasons could be drawn out and worked on, and certainly nobody identified a link between debriefing the kids properly and communication with the church.

The folks on University Heights were up for a trip to Tijuana, impressed with his interview in which he mentioned it often.

His ego was rattled and he left Ablaze badly. He told Garry and Ellen what stuck up frauds they were, sucking up to rich congregants and pandering to perception management protocols like some big corporation. There was enough truth in this to really smart, and Garry was troubled enough about the damage he might do with an attitude like that to pay him off for three months, require him to clear his desk and cease functioning as a staffer with immediate effect. His church email address was cancelled. Word got out that he was 'not in a great place and needed to be given some space.'

Garry of course very professionally led the 'sending out' ceremony as part of a Sunday service, repeating inwardly, 'say nice things, say nice things,' and smiling dazzlingly at Buzz. He led the church in prayer for Buzz's exciting new ministry asking him make sure he kept in good contact going forward.

He couldn't help seeing in his mind's eye the opening sequence from the mission trip video in which Buzz had given a silent interview through a rudely decorated van door with a crudely scrawled label. Very apt, he thought, very apt.

8.   MISUNDERSTOOD

Eve and Joseph discussed the possibility which had come through a visit from Steven Oudraogo, Regional Superintendent for the denomination.

Steven had suggested that Joseph consider an opportunity to study in England for a couple of years. The advantages of European study were many including the accessibility of excellent teachers from across Europe and North America but chiefly it would facilitate strategic European relationships. These were the kind of contacts that had so helped the late Michel Diama in his superb development of the church in which they had acted as understudies in Ouaga.

Money was very tight for the little church in Bandaradougou, and without external investment they would struggle to make much headway. Joseph and Eve had worked hard both to generate sufficient income to survive and to begin the process of discipleship with a community that had a long history of engagement with belief systems that were utterly at odds with the Gospel of Christ.

Issues such as pride and shame were virtues in Islamic animist traditions, but points of repentance in the kingdom of Jesus. Consulting and interaction with spirits was normal and laudable traditionally here, yet the bible instructed the abandonment of such things.

Joseph likened the early discipleship struggles in Bandaradougou to those he imagined the Apostle Paul had worked though two millennia earlier in Philippi. According to the New Testament his new congregation comprised of a rich textile merchant and her family, a formerly demon possessed fortune teller and a jailer who appeared to injure people for a living, his presumably brutalized family, plus possibly a few ex–cons.

Sayouba hung around the church and did odd jobs on the property, also helping out with their little patch of land. He ate with them and attached himself to their family. This gave them the opportunity to help him develop the necessary social skills for interaction with the wider community. It was also very draining until they were able to establish some boundaries, taking care to ensure he did not feel rejected by the process.

Eve was excited by the offer of European study and very keen that Joseph should pursue every opportunity at this stage of life. She was prepared to take a holding leadership role in his absence. Rather than leap at the chance though, they asked for some time to pray in order for them to test the matter before God. During that time both felt completely at peace regarding their motives and what they wanted to do with the strategic opportunities that would naturally follow. Their test was really, 'What would it mean for the people we are committed to serve?' They were less at peace about the practical arrangements. Eve in particular was terrified by the prospect of leading the church.

Aboubacar the chief had been a generous and positive support to the development of their little congregation and had himself made great strides as a rapidly maturing disciple of Christ. They asked him to take some responsibilities in the church, along with a number of other men and women who had gifts and characters tending towards leadership.

Steven had promised to return in time for the necessary arrangements to be made, at which point elders and leaders were installed to take the church forward under Eve's guidance in Joseph's absence.

Joseph soon found himself enjoying the bewildering and terrifying experience of making his first flight to Europe, happily with two other Burkinabe pastors for company. The others were both in their second year of studies in the UK.

Apparently the college had decided to invest in development of African pastors and had chosen Burkina Faso, with which one of the principals had strong links, as the focus of this investment. There was sufficient funding for only one fully sponsored student that year, and Joseph having been outstanding in the most prestigious denominational Bible College in Ouaga and part of a highly influential family had been a natural choice.

Air France had provided a wonderfully comfortable seat. In fact Joseph had never before sat in such a comfortable seat before and their food had been excellent. Joseph was too excited and stressed by the long journey to the airport and the unfamiliar processes he had to follow, to sleep or to be hungry.

Ouagadougou Airport was a one pace place. Nobody appeared to operate with any urgency, and their flight was late arriving. There was a delay in preparing the plane for departure and it was very late away. Nobody seemed concerned in the slightest about schedules.

Charles de Gaulle Airport in Paris was absolutely mind blowing for Joseph. He had never experienced architecture on this scale nor anything like the technology and systems which shepherded him through gates and scanners, up conveyors and along walkways. There was a vast crowding cacophony of unfamiliar images shouting for his attention, overloading his brain. He was grateful to God to whom he appealed for help several times, for providing the two fellow travelers as guides. Without them he felt he would surely have been completely lost.

His heavily accented French and lunging awkward movements seemed to him very conspicuously out of place and gauche among echoing halls filled with smart looking seasoned travelers patiently checking screens and watches and moving purposefully around in long lines.

They were met at Gatwick airport by a grinning staff member from the college, well known to his companions. The silent, exhausted Joseph headed for the rear right hand seat, furthest from the driver and therefore any possible inclusion in conversation. All talk in the car had been conducted in English making things very difficult for Joseph. The driver was from a place called Middlesborough and may as well have been speaking in Arabic from Joseph's perspective.

They arrived at the college, nestling in the greenest hills Joseph had ever seen, at 5.00 p.m. It was approximately 30 hours since he had set out from Bobo and was completely fatigued, so he could tell his brain was slow. He was shown to a room and greeted there by a smiling young lad, Giles who was to be his room mate. This fellow seemed very friendly but spoke quickly, making no attempt to accommodate his language limitations. He was from the West side of Britain. Joseph would later learn that he spoke with a thick rural accent.

'Are you tired?'

Joseph had enough English to understand the question and lacking confidence in actually speaking to an Englishman he decided to limit himself to yes and no answers initially.

He was tired, 'Yes.'

'OK, so that's your bed over there. You can unpack into this drawer unit and then I expect you'll want to get your head down. The toilets showers and wash basins are just along the corridor. I'll make sure I'm quiet when I come in later. Do you want some supper?'

Joseph didn't understand the question, what was this word supper? He decided that since he had already used the word yes, he would mix things up a bit.

'No.'

'OK, I guess you had something on the plane I'll get off down to the canteen then, they've rung the bell.' With that Giles left the room.

Joseph was left trying to understand this inhospitable culture where guests were not greeted with food. He was absolutely famished, and the air in the room was colder than any he'd experienced in his life. There was a chance that he might not survive this! He kept all his clothes on and had his first experience of attempting to sleep beneath a duvet. Happily he was too tired to remain awake and therefore hungry and cold for too long.

Life at the International Christian Training College (or ICTC as it was known to thousands of Pentecostal churches around the world) settled quickly into a strictly regimented programme not too dissimilar to that at his previous college in Ouaga, but with a lot less emphasis on preaching.

Food was very basic, which suited Joseph admirably; and tasteless, which did not. He thought back to the amazing meals Eve was able to produce from very meagre resources; fiery flavours, deep bitterness, rich aromas always from home grown or hand gathered ingredients. The day began well with porridge, thick and filling not too unlike millet saghbo but with very different sauces. Joseph developed a liking for jam. Lunch was soup and bread, and the evening meal was one of seven unvarying uninspiring low cost bulk catering recipes, cooked on rotation by a small team of students under supervision from an uncompromising chef.

Lectures were initially extremely difficult to follow and Joseph had to work very hard, especially in the early weeks. He found the lecturers were experienced at working with international classes.

Some, those based in mainland Europe, even slipped in some French explanations to complicated points.

Joseph was determined to excel at study and threw himself into college life with a wonderful attitude, willing to do whatever was asked and more besides. His room mate Giles was likewise highly motivated and in addition to classes and rostered domestic duties, seemed keen to spend his relaxation time making and fixing things. Pretty soon every fixture and fitting in the room and on their landing was working perfectly. Joseph watched him closely, held torches, passed tools and so on. He learned much about the workings of many of the myriad of mechanical objects in European buildings.

At the weekends some students returned to their homes and families. Those from overseas or from long distances away remained in college. Here the really firm friendships formed, and Joseph was amazed at the inclusion he enjoyed from the predominantly white fellow students. He had an ingrained deep respect of white folks. He could not say for certain why that was. Perhaps it was because of the colonial superiority exercised by the French. Possibly it was the deep veneration with which the American missionaries were held within his denomination of the church. It may even have been a culture of partiality normalized across the churches. Whites meant wallets, and wallets made great friends.

Whatever his reasons — cultural conditioning, educational inferiority, mechanical competence, work ethic perception perhaps — he did not expect to be one of the group. He was however totally included. His personality and contributions formed part of the whole dynamic from the inside. This was something ICTC did extremely well. Its staff team worked hard to foster brilliant relationships among and between students.

There was one piece of disillusionment for Joseph. He had expected his peers to be amazing young men and women of God. They were not. He found that at every turn some did their best to break the rules of the college, avoid giving of their best, tending to behave significantly more selfishly than he had imagined. These things were not true of his room mate, who was exceptional and with whom Joseph quickly formed a deep and trusting friendship.

As to the faith element visible and present in the college, here again there was something not quite up to the mark Joseph had been expecting. There were some great stories from the lecturers about things people had done, really inspiring things. There were not so many stories from the lives of the students. Many had no concept of the kind of tangible faith so normal and necessary for life in Burkina Faso.

The students struggled to pray for very long, when they did it was energy-less stuff. However when Antonio from Milan prayed for Joseph there were a definite signs of a bit more life.

'God is gonna increase you, he is gonna pour goodness upon you, he is gonna rain down blessing on your finances, on your family, on your home, on your body, he is gonna make you stronger, he is gonna make you wiser, no hair on your head will be harmed, you're not gonna live in want, you are marked for greatness, amen.'

Joseph felt encouraged.

Contact with Eve was impossible. He prayed for her every night and trusted God for her safety and for the growing community of believers in his church.

Christmas at college was an all-African affair. Everybody except the Africans went home. Joseph, Eduard and Joel were invited to Principal Robert's home for roast turkey. Joseph was overwhelmed by the kindness of this typically English family. Roast turkey was in his opinion the finest meal he had eaten in England, and warmed by an open fire, soporifically stuffed with food, he recalled this day as the most enjoyable of any he spent in England. Roast turkey remained forever his favourite Western food.

In the second term, with his English steadily improving, Joseph enquired about the possibility of taking a part time job at the weekends. He was hoping to earn some money to send back to Eve.

A McDonald's Restaurant was opening on the A23 between nearby Horley and Redhill, recruiting for those with no experience. There was almost full employment in the area and the chain was happy to take on a good looking African willing to do anything and happy to work Saturday nights. Resplendent in a brown and cream striped uniform complete with natty cap, Joseph soon learned to produce a steady stream of fries, to clear and wipe tables and to keep the bins empty and ketchup dispensers topped up.

The other employees found him something of an anomaly. He didn't like smutty jokes, didn't watch the TV and was never up for socializing with them. He worked really hard all the time, never ran anyone down and offered to pray for his colleagues at every opportunity. At first it was highly embarrassing. Someone needed to tell him that a Salfords McDonald's employee was willing to talk in detail about any showbiz gossip, anything going on in the town, who'd done what with and to whom, and even their own sex life. Spirituality however was completely taboo. In time he was put into perspective. He was seen as the sweet African guy who didn't really get it, looked well buff but wasn't up for a good time. They all loved him though, it was very hard not to.

He mostly enjoyed getting to know these locals, prayed for them every day and looked for ways of blessing and serving them. He did struggle slightly with the language, especially some of the innuendo and curse words that flew about. The pay was absolutely amazing, and he was able to save almost every penny because his living costs were found by his sponsor.

Not every part of the job was easy to pick up. Possibly because he was personable and friendly his supervisor decided to try him on the tills. He was given support to start with while he learned the ropes. He quickly grasped the basics, taking the money, calling the orders, fetching drinks and collating the items onto trays.

Problems only occurred when someone with a really thick accent ordered something unusual.

'I wanna plain double meal wiv large chips anna strawbry miwkshake anna Big Mac wivart the gherkin, mejum chips anna Fanta wiv no fizzy.'

'I am sorry I do not understand.'

'I said I wanna plain double meal wiv large chips anna strawbry miwkshake anna Big Mac wivart the gherkin, mejum chips anna Fanta no wiv fizzy.'

This did not make any more sense and Joseph flapped his fingers in helpless apprehension. He wanted so much to do well at this job, and he wanted to serve these people to a high standard.

'You stupid or summink?' The speaker had left school without any GCSEs above grade E, had never held a job, had four children each by different fathers and could barely speak her first language intelligibly. Joseph had gained a bachelors degree in divinity in his second language, French and was attempting to hold down a job in his fourth language. She didn't know anyone brighter than him.

'I am very sorry I did not understand your order and I cannot fetch it for you until I do. Perhaps you could say it one more time slowly.'

'God they get some crap in here! Oi!' to the girl at the neighbouring till, 'can you tell Thierry Henri here that I wanna plain double meal wiv large chips anna strawbry miwkshake anna Big Mac wivart the gherkin, mejum chips anna Fanta no wiv fizzy.' She laughed mockingly and assertively.

She got what she wanted, but wasn't finished yet. She hissed at Joseph, 'I don't know why you bovver comin' over 'ere, get back in your own country.'

He got that OK.

'Oh no miss, I have no intention of remaining in this country, when I have completed my education there is much to do where I live, many people to help. I am called to reach out to them with the love of God.'

'Well gawd 'elp em if you're on the case mate! I don't know, bloody religious nutters comin' over 'ere! Betcha one o' them muslins aintcha? Gonna blow us all up I 'spect. Have you got any barbecue and sweet chili? Oh don't bovver, I'll ask 'er.' She moved aside to the neighbouring till before flouncing weightily to a far table where she began to harangue her uncontrollable brood.

She left Joseph sweating and feeling disappointed that he wasn't doing too well. He comprehended most of that last bit. Happily this kind of thing happened only rarely and he was hoping that as his language skills improved he would do better. He looked at the desperate state of the woman and wondered how he could engage with her and begin to work on the pastoral issues that were so easy to read in her tone and persona. He had seen girls like this back home around the markets. Abused, neglected, brutalized, vicious. He wandered what had happened to her.

His thoughts took him back to Bobo market and then on to Bandaradougou. He was desperate to speak with Eve, to be with his people, to worship with a djembe, to get moving on some regeneration of his village to bring God's hope to his community.

At the end of the summer term there was no money from the sponsor to fly him back to Ouagadougou, and Joseph made a decision not to spend £1000 on travel, choosing to remain in the UK for the whole of his two year course. He helped out on the summer camps programme with Giles.

He sent all of his money, a sum of nearly £1900 with his friend Eduard back to Ouaga. Eduard's time at ICTC was complete and he was returning to the capital prior to being called to lead a church near Tenkodogo, to its South East.

Eduard faithfully paid in the money to the central denominational headquarters. It was destined for Eve and her struggling little church in Bandaradougou. Unfortunately after it had been paid in to the central funds, the audit trail went cold. No money appeared in Bandaradougou and there were insufficient records to track what had happened to it. Eve never saw a franc.

Summer in England was beautiful and as Joseph travelled down towards the Sussex coast he marveled again at the green rolling hills and patchwork fields of this beautiful Island. The spreading oak trees in particular with their craggy bark and gnarled deformities caught his eye; witnesses to hundreds of years of attrition by the constantly changing weather.

Attrition and constantly changing weather aptly summed up Joseph's experience of summer in England. It was extremely cold and very wet. Living in tents was fun and sleeping close to the ground outdoors slightly reminiscent of life in Djigouera. He was very glad of the time spent on camp. Without it he would not have picked up on some assumptions which were the default position towards crafting programmes for young people within the British Pentecostal church culture and were almost altogether absent in his own.

The camp rules were very clearly explained and each young person was expected to remain within them. That much was very similar. If the rules were broken a set of sanctions could be applied by the leaders to ensure fair compliance by all and a safe, just mini–community could function. Again that was very similar, except that the leaders here did not beat the children. The main departure from the norms he had experienced in Ouaga (when helping with youth events while training) were to do with crafting the whole programme around the styles and preferences of young people. This was an absolutely fundamental difference.

In Ouaga, camps for young people had taken an assumption that their primary *raison d'être* was to edify the children of Christians. There were no Christian camps for children of other faiths or none back home.

The assumption in his home country was that an agenda calling young people up to adult friendly study and worship would be wholly helpful and appropriate for kids. The outcome of going with an adult orientated agenda was that the young people were kind of glad to go and to appear keen to participate and to please the leaders with their engagement. They were also bored out of their skulls much of the time, with teaching that made no effort whatsoever to link to how they best received information, or what they most wanted to do. Any interactivity was limited to rhetorical questions and drawing dutiful hallelujahs from them periodically, as preachers assailed them vigourously with hectoring tones of animated excitement.

Here at the British summer camps he found the agenda blended two questions: 'What do young people enjoy doing?' and, 'What do we think it is important do with them if they are to thrive in their spiritual, social, physical and emotional development?'

This was a refreshing approach and as he watched young people of little or no Christian commitment begin to or continue to engage with the things of God without the need for coercion or haranguing he felt he had seen something he could take home.

9.   COMING ALIVE

Eve had decided that she would not try to emulate Joseph's style of leadership in his absence. She could not be him, but she had strengths and it was around these that she would have to focus her efforts. She was filled with love for the people. Drawn from the well of her intimacy with God, it bore with offences and grievances. It covered over issues that would normally divide. It was a persevering, hoping, self–denying, uplifting force for good, flowing in her and through her.

She was careful to continually build friendships that were filled with trust and tried to make sure that everything she did was first weighed against the principle of, 'Does this fit within the framework of the love of God for me and the people I serve?'

She felt a little like a widow, and drew strongly on the experiences gained through Florence's leadership after the murder of Philippe.

There were immediate difficulties with the men. None of them had ever been led by a woman before; particularly not an attractive one. Eve carried an air of dignity and genteel strength. She could not relax, let her hair down and belly laugh with the team as Joseph would do; allowing his personality and drive to bring a natural easily understood leadership dynamic. To do that as a woman alone just would not have worked in this scenario.

She had instead to rely on a determination to be filled with God's third self, his Spirit, promised to all who asked for him.

'Him?' reflected Eve, as she grew to understand more about the nature of God. From her perspective the Spirit of God appeared more to carry the roles whose image was most naturally reflected in women. The Spirit of God nurtures, draws alongside and helps, teaches, prompts and reminds. Probably most definitively 'he' gives birth — there's a trick for a male to pull off, she pondered. True, he testifies and he convicts, creates and, in the case of some of those Old Testament characters, does a fair bit of confronting and battling. There was clearly more to God than one human gender could accurately reflect, she mused. She was, in her role, quite naturally reflecting some of the more feminine properties of God.

It was in welcoming, honouring, depending and relying upon the Spirit of God that Eve drew most comfort in her ministry and most encouragement in her leadership.

Her particular forte was in leading and facilitating intercession; gathering the church to sustained corporate prayer. Eve called the church to pray every Thursday night from 7 p.m. until midnight. The village was without electricity thus prayer was conducted around a fire built in the church compound. This had the double attraction of providing light and, because the wood burnt was invariably eucalyptus, it deterred biting insects from joining their fellowship.

Eve explained to the church members, some principles for their vigils when she first enthusiastically gathered the congregation for these times spent crying to God together for intervention in their circumstances.

'The authority of any meeting is limited by two things. First, the mandate it is given by the governance structure in which it

sits. Second, the power of its leader to drive through the implementation of any decisions made.'

She could hear the voice of Philippe in her head as she repeated his teaching.

'That is the beauty of corporate prayer. The governance structure in which it sits is the Kingdom of God. The meeting is a place where the body, the church, meets with its head, the King. The decisions agreed in this context cannot be stopped. It is the most powerful assembly possible. Those brought alive by the Spirit of God in session with the Son of God have this invitation from the Father: "It shall be done for them".'

She encouraged, 'It is a dynamic to be experienced rather than described.'

The little church had many things to bring before the Father, to be 'done for them'. Medical issues here, because of limited resources and the lack of availability of clinical services were often brought into their prayer times. Harvest yields, and therefore rain on time and in plenty; so vital to the survival of the families, featured much. They prayed for Joseph in his studies. They prayed for their own business in the local markets, for good sales and favour among the traders; and for the strength to stand firm in acting justly and rightly in their business transactions. There were employment needs for youngsters who could not all be deployed in the fields. And there was the desperate need for a teacher and a school.

These were the needs of the immediate community, but Eve thought often, especially during the prayer vigils, about young girls like herself. She had not forgotten her promise to God that if he rescued her, she would help others. Every night hundreds of girls like her would be sleeping on little patches of dirt, with no idea about hygiene or nutrition. No education, no prospects, and no future beyond abject poverty and early death. 'Dear God,' she prayed many times, 'help us bring change.'

It was on a Thursday night at around 7.30 p.m. that they carried Axelle into the compound. The vigil was under way though people tended to drift in over the first hour as with most of their meetings. Eve was at first unaware of the presence of the little family as she focused on God and tried to discern what was on his mind for them. Then she saw what was happening.

Axelle was a young girl aged nine. She was suffering from a high fever and had been sick for a nearly one week. Her little form was limp, her breathing shallow and ragged. She was very far gone and her father, deeply concerned laid her on a blanket asking, 'Please, Mama Eve, help us!' The mother stood a little way back, shy and uncertain of what might happen. Neither parent had had any previous contact with the church; they had walked four miles from the neighbouring village of Boulon–Bossie.

Eve was quick to point out that any help Axelle would receive could only come from God, but they would be pleased to pray for her. She placed her hand lightly on Axelle's cheek; it was burning hot.

It was not unusual for people to ask for prayer, but nobody had been carried into a vigil night before. Eve saw the little girl and her anxious father and mother as God's agenda for her prayer time tonight.

The leaders were all there with Eve, she looked around the ring of worshippers in the firelight, picking out these key people from among the others. Aboubacar with his big booming voice, his wife Aminata also big and strong voiced; a formidable sight in the markets. Mohammed and Issouf, brothers still living on their father's bountiful land with its orchard of mango trees. Their generosity to families struggling to survive the annual famines was well known and deeply valued by the community's poor. Daoud the Fulani who had been wonderfully healed from a paralysed hand and joyfully joined the church only to be horribly beaten by members of his family. He faced daily persecution for colluding with villagers, with whom his family would have no dealings following years of mutual suspicion and animosity.

These were her leaders, and she could not have hoped for better, more determined fellow disciples of Christ with whom to take forward the Gospel.

She asked the church to call on God for little Axelle and made sure that the sick girl was shielded from the warmth of the fire. She was not covered and her mother crept close to her, using a damp cloth to wipe her face.

For half an hour the worshippers in turn cried out to God. They shouted as if their volume might awaken him. Eve smiled. It was good to hear their passion and desire to help the little girl. They were giving this their best. She asked for quiet and requested that the elders lay hands on the little girl. Eve had a little jar of oil that was used to anoint the sick in church services. She was ready to pour some on the girl now, but as she touched her she noticed she was very still and much cooler. She placed her ear to Axelle's mouth and could detect no breathing. The little girl's mother noticed her actions and asked anxiously what she was doing.

'I am afraid she is not breathing,' said Eve.

The mother quickly knelt down beside her little girl and checked for herself, noticing her cooling body, listening for her heart, drawing close to detect her breath, hoping desperately for something, anything. There was nothing, she was gone. There was a little shudder of acceptance and disappointment from the mother. The father's arms hung limply for a moment, then he held his wife and they looked down helplessly at the little girl.

Sadly, the sight of dead children was common enough in these villages, and many present had held their own dead offspring. There was a very strong feeling of empathy around the glowing fire.

The father picked up Axelle and carried her into the church. The sight of her, tiny forlorn and dead, lying on the crude table at the front, lit by flickering candles caused a powerful wave of grief to overcome Eve. She turned to the parents: 'We will now pray for you.' Hers was a flat hopeless voice; the defeated lackluster utterance of disappointment and failure.

They left the little girl in the church for the remainder of their prayer time, the parents returned home to prepare their little household for a traditional burial. It was agreed that the family would send the girl's uncle to collect the body later in the night. In the meantime Sayouba would keep watch.

It was as the group gathered round mum and dad before they left, and Aboubabcar began a great, sobbing, heart rending anguished prayer of grief and empathy that Eve felt a sense of anger and indignation come upon her rising within her spirit. This was the church God had given her to serve and tend. It had been disgraced by failing this dear little family in their hour of need. Where there should have been a demonstration of the mighty power of God, joy and excitement; there was bereavement and sorrow.

Eve took a moment to assess what was happening within her. She was a realist who had lost many people before. She knew when it was time to give up, and generally when you're dealing with a body, it was time to give up. Again as she thought about the way things had gone she was overcome with anger at the outrage of losing the child during a prayer vigil. She took a decision based on a mixture of her feelings, objective observation of the situation and its context and discernment based on what she had read in the bible and seen and heard in her experience of church.

'We will pray again for the girl.' There was much more determination in her voice, strength beyond her own was rising within her.

The vigil refocused its prayer for the little girl and somehow retained its focus and its effort until it was time to go home at midnight. Almost without daring to hope, Eve led the people down to where Sayouba sat quietly beside the little body. Axelle was stiff. Rigor mortis had begun to set in. There was a flat finality to the situation and for the second time that night Eve felt the sting of hopeless defeat, the sense of disappointment this time with the additional despair of being completely wrong.

As she turned to leave the church she felt a palpable wave of anger come over her again. This really was not her own passion rising and she went with it.

'We will not stop praying,' she declared, 'we will go on until they come to collect the body.'

Her people faithfully followed her lead as she led them beyond logic, beyond hope, beyond recovery of credibility if she was wrong. She led them into faith, responding to the presence of the Holy Spirit within her and holding to the strength he gave her.

Everyone was already exhausted and Eve was emotional, spent. Two hours later she had cried her tears dry. Finished, her energy and her ability to frame words was gone. The only thing left was the unbreakable spirit within her. The spirit her father had admired and hated. As she had wrestled for the life of the little girl she had found words coming that were not in her language. Of course she'd been taught to speak in tongues and had actually kind of picked it up from others around her not really sure if she was just babbling or was actually speaking a language. That was part of being a Pentecostal.

This night was different. Great tearing groans and flowing speech had come to her. Her people too had experienced things previously not seen as their determination to stick with her in this most anguished of vigils had run and run. She wondered if maybe the answer to the question, 'What does God want to do here?' was more complicated than heal the little girl.

The child's uncle came for the girl at a quarter to four. Nobody had gone home. He entered the church and found the girl as silent as before but breathing, fever gone, very weak, but very much alive.

That was the beginning of a time of mixed blessing for the little church in Bandaradougou. First and probably more importantly, a great many people from the neighbouring village of Boulon–Bossie joined the church, including of course little Axelle and her mum and dad. The growth did not stop there. Other villages in the vicinity caught word of what had happened. The little church started getting curious visitors, keen to see some miracles. They represented both an opportunity for growth, and a nuisance.

There was another reaction to the event which was just a nuisance. People started sending Eve stiffs from all over the place. She fully understood, people were desperate and they had heard what had happened. Carts started appearing with corpses. This wasn't great as some of them had been dead a while and stank.

She sent the bodies back with a mixture of compassion and clarity: 'Only God can raise the dead, and in my experience he usually does not. If you want him to get involved in this matter, you must ask him yourself.'

Eve was very certain that the initiative for persevering in prayer for Axelle had come from the Spirit of God and not from her. She was equally clear that to suggest she could raise the dead was utter nonsense. Her part in the events of the raising of Axelle had been to be available, to be listening to what she truly believed God was saying. Then with a fairly clear indication of what he was asking her to do, to find just enough faith for him to be glorified through her cooperation.

Oh, she had run the matter through her mind many times. She was convinced that any learning she could take forward from the experience was that there was some kind of synergy between obedience, character and availability. There seemed to be room in the dynamic of relationship between her and God for negotiation, spontaneity, divine initiative and her obedience. She could half understand, as if she had caught a glimpse of something and lost sight just before she could focus properly.

The lasting impact the matter had on Eve, quite apart from a wonderful friendship with Axelle was a deep and wonderful excitement about God. He was bigger than she'd thought, closer than she'd realized. There would not come a time now when Eve would wonder about her identity as a Christian leader. God had written something permanent on the deepest most intimate part of her heart: 'I hear you, you are mine, I am with you, I love you.'

She took forward from that day a surety of step in walking with God, and a sense of identity as his beloved daughter which together would prove to be a powerful combination.

In the absence of Joseph, completely exposed to the challenges of scratching a living and leading a church Eve had the curious awareness of coming alive. It had to do she supposed with being compelled by circumstances to draw very close to the source of all life.

10. SMALL BEGINNINGS

For his second year at the college Joseph changed roommate and found himself holed up with Antonio, someone who on the face of it appeared a lively and fun fellow student.

He found Antonio an interesting character. He came from the Napoli coast, an apparently very beautiful part of Italy, where the lemons in the hillside groves grew as large as grapefruits, and the blues of sea went from turquoise to Indigo around the white volcanic rock.

Antonio was very keen to pray for people. Joseph imagined that at some stage in his past Antonio had been very blessed by some ministry time. Whatever the reason, whenever he prayed for people, it was always with the same prayer:

'God is gonna increase you, he is gonna pour goodness upon you, he is gonna rain down blessing on your finances, on your family, on your home, on your body, he is gonna make you stronger, he is gonna make you wiser, no hair on your head will be harmed, you're not gonna live in want, you are marked for greatness, amen.'

Joseph recalled the first time Antonia had prayed for him. He had been much encouraged, and had felt that he'd encountered someone with some faith and some passion.

Faith and passion were not things he could readily identify in Antonio. There was a deal of excitement. Joseph would have called it enthusiasm but he'd learnt the in introduction to Greek studies that enthusiasm was derived from the term 'full of God' — and that he was not.

Antonio came alive when an excitable preacher or speaker called for a response from his audience. He spent a lot of time playing 'Snake' on his Nokia mobile, something he tended to do in lectures as well as during free time. He was less alive whenever there were duties to be done, and would often ask Joseph to fill in for him while he ran some important errand, or caught up with something vital, or just needed to talk to someone about something really urgently. Joseph was happy to do this. He enjoyed working as part of the team, and life at the college was a lot easier than back in Bandaradougou, every day was a blessing. He was glad to do extra as an expression of gratitude.

In discussion times and focused prayer times where the students wrestled with issues or God, Antonio was largely a silent spectator, becoming far more animated and conversational between lessons and meetings.

Joseph observed Antonio disengaging himself from the material of the course, becoming increasingly like someone marking time. It was not long before they had said everything they could to one another, and communication became confined to the necessities of cohabitation. This was in marked contrast to the laughter, pranks and deep discussion late into the night he'd enjoyed with Giles. The few things Joseph did know were that Antonio came from a moderately successful church which was led by his uncle, and had been sent to Bible College with a view to joining the leadership team. He was a big soccer fan and had a poster of Diego Maradonna in the colours of his beloved Napoli above his bed in their room. He was a good player too. Football was one of the few topics which brought him to life.

Antonio would spend quite a lot of time off site at the weekend, mainly to go and watch football in nearby Reigate sometimes stretching the rules a little especially regarding lights out times. He had a way of entering the building after it was locked and often slipped quietly back to the room after midnight doing his best not to disturb Joseph. He unmistakably smelled of alcohol when he returned, which was a breach of the college's rules during term time. In Burkina Faso, for a Pentecostal pastor to take alcohol would mean the end of their ministry.

It had been something of a surprise to Joseph to discover that most European Christians drink alcohol. In fact drinking was openly encouraged, and taught. One of the lecturers had quipped, 'Some of our churches appear to wish to re–write the bible and have Jesus turning wine into water to sober up a wedding for his first miracle.'

Giles and the others certainly liked to drink and spoke of it often. Joseph was very impressed with Giles, and had to admit that there was no evidence that his 'sinful' drinking affected his ministry. Slowly, awkwardly, a traditional spiritual 'given' in the tapestry of Joseph's experience of church culture began to unravel. It became clear to him that what the New Testament portrayed was not what he believed. He believed and accepted some things because they had been instilled into his Christian culture by giants like Louis Oudraogo who were right on so many counts, that it was taken that they were right on all.

He resolved as much as possible going forward, to assess what the bible had to say and especially the behaviour that Jesus demonstrated as of prior importance when it came to setting behaviour standards for his own leadership team and the community culture they sought to create.

He did not begin to drink alcohol however. He simply understood why others did so and that they enjoyed it. He could not afford it and did not want to start doing something which back in Africa would not be understood and could lead to his rejection.

All was not well with Antonio, Joseph could tell, but with no real depth to their conversation, and Antonio very quick to shut down any serious talk, it was impossible to discern what was going on with him or how to help him, if he wanted help. His interests were so clearly outside of the college curriculum that Joseph began to wonder why he was in training at all, and why the ICTC had accepted him.

Joseph found the sneaking around and deliberate breach of college rules extremely serious, and wrestled with what to do. He wanted to be loyal to Antonio but he must also be faithful to him. Helping to conceal issues that really needed to be dealt with would be loyal but unfaithful. Joseph resolved to speak with the college authorities, and matters came to a head when he mentioned what was happening at the weekends to the college staff member who had responsibility for his pastoral care, Stuart.

Stuart thanked Joseph and investigated the matter by following Antonio into Reigate the following weekend. He had been disturbed to observe not only a breach of the college rules concerning drinking and returning late, but also two hours spent at a sleazy looking hotel with a girl who was clearly working in the sex industry.

Antonio was invited to Stuart's office for a discussion about conduct on the Monday. Stuart wasn't good at confrontation, and would go to great lengths to avoid it if possible. Normally dealing with Bible College students saw him at worst reminding people of their responsibilities towards the duty rotas. Occasionally he would have to deal with outbursts linked to the claustrophobia of community life. Once or twice he had caught the rough edge of an aggrieved parent or church leader whose expectations of what the college could or would provide were too high.

The matters arising with Antonio were so far off the scale of Stuart's experience or expectations from a disciplinary viewpoint that he had panicked, hardly even daring to think clearly about the implications of what he had seen. He was badly prepared, had no evidence beyond his observations and no other witness. He had confided in nobody and was isolated, exposed.

Antonio's response had been denial, even in the face of an eye witness. Furthermore he had threatened Stuart at a level that was again beyond the reach of his imagination. Antonio claimed to be connected to the mafia and explained to Stuart that if any of the accusations made privately in their conversation went any further, then he would arrange for Stuart to meet an unfortunate end.

Stuart was a gentle fellow, quiet, loving and generous. He had not been exposed at any time in his life to criminal activity. He avoided violent films, unpleasant people and if he did come across unsavoury behaviour would hope someone else would deal with it. Here he was totally out on a limb and reliant on his own pluck and character. There wasn't much of either for him to draw on.

The interview ended suddenly with Antonio shouting half in Italian, very threatening, glaring malevolently at him. He then left the room in terrible furious silence. Stuart was truly traumatized. He spent a few minutes unable to think straight, his hands trembling uncontrollably, his heart beating rapidly, breathing fast. He was close to tears and absolutely terrified.

He did almost nothing, internalizing the stress. He checked in with Joseph a couple of weeks later who was pleased to say that Antonio had not been offsite at all lately. Stuart consoled himself over his own paralysis with the fact that Antonio had changed his behaviour following Stuart's courageous challenge, and that there was therefore no need to take matters further.

Antonio left the college at Christmas, his studies incomplete, stating that the course did not really give him what he needed with how he wanted his ministry to go. At his farewell meal held towards the end of term he prayed for all of his fellow students:

> 'God is gonna increase you, he is gonna pour goodness upon you, he is gonna rain down blessing on your finances, on your

family, on your home, on your body, he is gonna make you stronger, he is gonna make you wiser, no hair on your head will be harmed, you're not gonna live in want, you are marked for greatness, amen.'

Stuart was so stressed by the Antonio matter that he had to take some sick leave. He never mentioned to anyone what had happened. Antonio returned to his family and their church without the qualification he had sought. Having gained some theological grounding and completed most of the course he joined the staff team of the church as a youth worker.

• • •

Joseph's work at Salfords McDonald's continued and as his language skills improved so it became much easier for him to play a decent role in the team. There were fewer racist incidents, possibly because he didn't invite them so easily.

His second year of study came more easily too, for the same reason. There were two assignments he was required to produce which he would find helpful for the remainder of his ministry life.

The first was a commentary on Religion. The students had to comment on the statement: 'Buddhism, Hinduism, Islam, Judaism, Christianity: five fingers of the same hand.'

His essay scored his highest grade for the entire course and asserted that the statement was probably true in that at a level of organized religion all were subject to the same corrupting and damaging influences of their leaders as the political systems they straddled. He included in his piece a critique of secular humanism, which when allied to advances in scientific technology was in his opinion the most efficient and destructive troublemaker of all the belief systems he'd looked at.

In conclusion he wrote, 'The naïvety that made this statement was born in ignorance. Until adequate understanding and criticism is invited and given to the claims of these and other major religions and belief systems, there is no chance for the peace it appears to promote.'

The second assignment, for which he did a tremendous amount of reading, invited comment on another statement: 'Christian leaders should stay out of politics.'

His was a fascinating perspective. He spoke as an African whose home village had for five centuries blended Islam and Animism influenced by shamanism, then had accepted a mystical iconic Catholicism, more latterly to be impacted and utterly transformed by Pentecostal disciples of Jesus motivated by selfless love. He argued that his nation had been subdued and governed just 100 years previously by the French with their colluding Catholicism. He also held that much of the poverty and injustice his people endured was linked to beliefs based in the Asian, central African and Middle Eastern systems which had influenced the population and its governance for 1000 years.

The advance of Islam, resisted until the 15th century by the Mossi Kingdoms had finally achieved whole scale conversions through the marriage of prosperous Muslim traders to significant Mossi women. Some of their offspring inherited chieftainships and enforced whole scale conversion on their people. This conversion route via parents each of whom held wholly differing beliefs had left the nation with a veritable alloy of Animism and Islam. The compromises which had taken place within the families had adapted the religions themselves.

He saw the many conquests of African nations and kingdoms to have been dominated by structures and agreements arranged to develop wealth and power. Worship was used to perpetuate or impose those structures and agreements. There was little respect for the intrinsic value of each individual to choose relationship with God or gods.

He was able to comment upon the contrast between radical Christian discipleship characterized by unconditional selfless love, and the fundamentalist religious radicalization associated with any organized religion including Christianity. This latter had

157

frequently displayed its character in violent obliteration of its opponents. He saw religions, including Christianity, as the projection onto a religious backdrop of the broken fallen characters of selfish men; especially their lust for power, influence and control.

In working on the second assignment, he identified a further piece of faulty Spiritual DNA back in his own denomination of the church. While tracking the link between the French colonialists and the Catholic Church, he explored the approach to politics of dear old Walter Lee and his friends from the Pentecostal movement. They had reacted badly to what they saw as the Catholic Church's collusion in political domination. Corruption was openly visible in the political system and the abuse of power was present both in government and the Catholic Church at that time. For laudable reasons his denominational pioneers had worked hard on ensuring that their aspiring young leaders steered well clear of what they viewed as a murky political trap.

This approach had left the country bereft of vigorous talented Pentecostal Christian leaders entering the political arena. It was an ill thought–through knee jerk reaction to a transient problem; and it denied the authentic activity of the Spirit of God.

Leaders determined to live in obedience to God ought to be able to enter a place of corruption and cleanse it rather than be overcome by it themselves. The pages of scripture demonstrated both: failure, Joseph as Prime Minister of Ancient Egypt; and success, Daniel as Prime Minister of Babylon.

The result of this second assignment would bring significant change his approach to the development of leaders within his own community.

He became determined to be among those carrying a fresh political agenda to his movement when he returned to Burkina Faso. He was convinced for example that polygamy was utterly destructive to family life, especially to the adequate nurture of children, to the economy and to the role of women in society.

He could track its elimination from God's people as the pages of scripture unfolded. At the time of Abraham way back at the beginning of the Old Testament when God began his story of intervention, polygamy appeared to be part of the normal human condition. By the time of the Apostles' writings in the New Testament in the first century AD the advance of justice through the Gospel of Jesus had begun to address it.

To remove polygamy from his country it would be necessary to bring a challenge to political leaders whose religious systems and traditions and preferences all had vested interests in its perpetuation. With an absence of Christian leaders' voices in government, this and many other injustices against which the good news of Jesus spoke so clearly would continue to form the fabric of his society, unchallenged by his church.

Joseph left the UK in late July. He took with him a post graduate diploma In applied theology, a notebook full of contacts many of whom who led or would one day lead churches all over Europe, £3000 saved from his work in McDonald's, and an understanding of Europeans which would be vital in collaboration for the remainder of his ministry life.

• • •

Ouagadougou had changed substantially even in the two short years since he had last been there. The Chinese and the Koreans were investing heavily in Burkina Faso. There were new roads, the city was visibly larger and there were many more vehicles, especially private cars, than before.

The bus journey down to Bobo–Dioulasso was significantly more comfortable than previously, as both the road surface and the vehicles had been upgraded. The market at Boromo half way along the highway was much the same, except that there were significantly more buses.

Reunion with Eve was tearful and ecstatic. Both partners had undergone extraordinary changes in the time of their separation. They looked into one another's eyes unable to know where to start with describing their experiences. There was too much and their overwhelming joy made speech a joy and a jumble. Each was anxious to see the joy of recognition and delight in the other's eyes. They were not disappointed.

He was full of questions about her safety and health, how the little house had survived the rains, how she had coped leading the church, wanting updates on the villagers' lives, especially those in the congregation. She wanted to know what it was like to fly. How was the cold and what was the food like? She had heard that both were awful. She listened intently to his descriptions of life in college. He told her about snow, and cricket, and youth camps, porridge and McDonald's.

Despite their long abstinence, the flames of passion burned low that night, he was tired from 30 hours on the road, but not beyond resurrection, she however was anxious that he should rest.

The welcome back service on Sunday was something of a shock. He had left a congregation of 91 including children. He returned to a church of 250 plus, enthusiastically worshiping and clearly both enjoying being together and eager to participate in dynamic relationship with God. The majority of his congregation didn't know him. One third of them came from another village altogether.

With the church well led by an effective team and growing strongly, Joseph had a firm platform from which to develop projects in the community. He was very keen to try to move the school closer to existence.

He spent money on improving the village water supplies, and cement for bricks to build a home for himself and his wife which would not wash away every four or five years.

Eve waited a few months before bringing up the subject of girls like herself, something burning within her.

> 'I remember calling to God to help when my mum died. I was in such despair and I could see the future for me and for my

children was without hope unless God rescued me. For a long time after that I did not think he had heard me, but now more than twelve years later I know that he did rescue me.

'I made a promise to him that if I got out of the hopeless tangle my family was in I would come back for girls like me. I want to do that Joseph, and every night when I lie down I think of them. Thousands and thousands of girls like me, growing up in terrible hunger and poverty and lack. No education, no understanding even of how it might be possible to escape. And they will give birth to girls who will live and die the same way. I cannot stand it Joseph. I cannot stand the pain of knowing and I must honour my promise to God.'

There are times when a husband makes a good call, and despite the very many things that were vying for his attention immediately around the little church, Joseph decided that his leadership team should take some time to think and to pray with Eve about what God might want from them. Especially he was keen to know how to support Eve whom God may have called for some other purpose than that of leading the church.

The team met and as he always did, Joseph led them in a time of mutual confession. There were no secrets in the room. This was a place of mutual trust. They knew about each other's weaknesses, what they were each dealing with. They all knew for example that Mohammed and Issouf struggled every day to remain generous. They wanted cars and electricity. They desired air conditioning and TV. However all around them people depended upon their wealth for survival.

The leadership team knew that Eve and Joseph were in agony over the reality that they were not producing children. That every prayer they prayed was in the context of God saying no to the one prayer they most wanted answered. They were aware that every month when Eve had her period she felt an utter failure. The sound of a baby crying, the joy of a parent laughing with a child, dedicating babies in the church; all sent daggers into her wounded heart. She would find some space to weep when these things overwhelmed her. They knew that Joseph still handled the situation as if it would end soon enough. He was frustrated, but there was a growing sense of despair and he had reached the point of not daring to hope.

They were all aware that Daoud struggled to forgive his family, and on a bad day wanted to hack to death with his machete those who threw stones at him. Aboubacar had been brought up a brute, and when angry had a tendency to hit his family. Aminata had a lot to forgive, and was doing her best.

These were the big rocks beneath the surface that the power of God was helping to clear or to break up. There were many others and new issues surfaced all the time.

They met before God in the context of understanding their need of his power even to overcome their weaknesses and disappointments. They knew that if there were problems between them these would affect the way they engaged with God's agenda. They were in agreement that forgiveness and honesty were necessary in this group if they were to be able to make good decisions.

The team discussed Eve's account of her personal journey. They spent 30 minutes alone and apart some walking, others, sitting quietly. They were called together again by Joseph and each in turn described what had been happening in their minds and hearts as they had been alone with God.

There was total peace in all of their spirits and as they reconvened each spoke of a growing warmth towards the matter. Since the aim of the project was to produce women of substance able to trade, they decided to call it Lydia Girls.

They agreed that Eve's life had taken a change of direction since she had prayed for help and they were agreed about the things which had happened to and for her as God had rescued her. In order to plan what should be in place to help others and their potential offspring out of the cycle of poverty, they decided to set up a pathway that mirrored hers.

They recalled that in spending time with Florence, Eve had learned to read and to handle basic mathematics. She had also been fed a better diet at least once a week, and had begun to understand nutrition. She had received clothes that had made her feel better about herself.

In time she had learned to make baskets, and had become able to trade, picking up her skills mainly through intuition. She had married a man who had no intention of taking additional wives. Throughout the process of escape to a completely transformed life she had received some help but the determination to make it had come from within her.

She had made a considerable effort to form a tangible relationship with God. This included researching what pleased, rather than appeased him; there was a subtle but important difference between the God of her mother's faith and the gods of her father's beliefs. She had experimented and prayed prayers of engagement, taking the time to reflect on what his response had been. What she had was real and tangible and affected her whole being.

They made a list of the transforming things:

- ✓ literacy;
- ✓ numeracy;
- ✓ nutrition advice and improved diet;
- ✓ decent clothing;
- ✓ learning a trade, and how to conduct business as a trader;
- ✓ Christian discipleship;
- ✓ self–esteem, and discernment regarding choice of husband.

The list was simple enough, but building a programme for girls that delivered it and persuading a family to release a girl into that programme with these goals for her would require patient conversation and explanation with the parents. The goals would be very different from the family's experiences and expectations.

Joseph's thoughts had been drawn to the biblical passage where Moses is asked, 'What is in your hand?' by God. God had used what was in his hand to do extraordinary things. The team decided to embark on this adventure with what was in their hands.

Aboubacar allocated a reasonable plot of land on which to build a little structure. Eve and Joseph made available a small proportion of their dwindling Macdonald's cash reserves. The matter was put before the church and a special offering taken. The result was not overwhelming but it was enough to think about working with eight girls and building an 18 by 18 foot classroom with a mud floor and plenty of shutter windows. They attached a washroom with a long–drop toilet and an area for showering. Several buckets and a jug for pouring water were supplied. Water for the shower buckets would have to be drawn from the village well. There was no plumbing and while the village did now have electricity, it did not reach to this property.

There was a significant sacrifice for their village in helping girls located further away from the city. They still had no school of their own, and this facility would focus on young people beyond the age of schooling. Most children in primary education left school at sixth grade if they made it that far. There were very few secondary schools, and entrance to them was expensive and required very good grades, normally unachievable in state primary education.

All the while they still had no school their children's futures were limited. However the leaders of the church were more drawn to what they believed God was saying than to immediate obvious needs. Those matters were not dropped from their agenda, nor dropped from their prayers, they just moved down the priority list. It made no sense, just seemed like what God wanted.

Joseph reminded the team that bad decisions could easily be reversed. Decisions made for bad reasons or bad motives were much harder to rectify. The key question in matters of discernment and decision making he said were not so much, 'Is this the right decision to make?' but rather, 'Are we making this decision for the right reasons?'

Joseph had been blessed with a gift from a retiring missionary called Robert, from the USA. He was being recalled to the US and no longer had need of his battered old Isuzu Trooper. He'd left a small cash reserve for maintenance, but there was very little money available for fuelling the vehicle.

Their first recruitment drive took place the following June. Eve and Joseph took the Isuzu to Djigouera where they stayed with Florence for a few days. They had visited a few times since leaving for Ouaga. The weddings of two of her sisters, and one brother had meant mandatory attendance. However since Joseph had been out of the country they neither of them had been able to come to their home village.

Ibrahim had aged and seemed much smaller than she recalled him. Dina looked very haggard, the effects of years of privation and suffering were written on her face. The old compound was tidy enough. The main family players now were Eve's oldest brother David and his wife. Dina and her kids were pulling their weight, but the inheritance would go to Eve's brother David. It would be for him to decide how to use the space for the wider family. Eve was very glad to see evidence of Christian discipleship in the way he was honouring his father and step mother.

Joseph and Eve shared the last of Joseph's McDonald's earnings with Ibrahim and Florence. Florence returned the money and requested that it be given to David to help him take care of Ibrahim. The church community cared very well for her and she was aware that in Ibrahim's compound there was significant need.

Joseph and Eve discussed their plan to help some of the village girls to gain a better life, eventually back in this village but after a transformative process, residentially in Bandaradougou. One problem they anticipated having was that of credibility. They had no track record of success, and they were comparatively poor themselves. It was an issue which they hoped would be better resolved in the village of their birth than anywhere else. Here at least, they were known as decent people.

They were very out of date in their understanding of the fortunes shifts and changes which had happened over the last few years in Djigouera. Florence was able to update them and agreed that their plan to avoid the children of church members unless in exceptionally hard circumstances, would help target the kids most at risk and currently out of reach of the loving church community.

Their own village was certainly the best place to start. They found that several of the families were only too pleased to release a hungry mouth to them, especially that of a girl. Many of the families also had servant girls. These were the children of relatives whose original family was too poor to feed them. The child would move to the new family and work as a servant for food to survive. Such children were often sexually abused, even hired out, as well as beaten and used as a slave. No family would want their child in this situation. Those who had to do it did not do so out of choice. Joseph and Ibrahim presented a far better option for such families.

The month of June was always a pressure month for the families, especially in the villages where subsistence cropping was the lifestyle of the majority. June was the month in which children began to starve and families ate less often, trying to make their food last through until harvest while preserving sufficient grain for planting.

Joseph and Eve left Djigouera with eight small nervous girls aged between twelve and fifteen loaded into the Isuzu. Eve was emotionally ragged, feeling too full to speak as her long held dream and prayer began to take shape. She was also experiencing waves of terror and feelings of inadequacy. Of course she knew how to care for children; she had cared for her siblings and for Dina's kids as part of her upbringing. Eight was a big task though.

The girls were excited, and the vehicle was filled with the jabber of eight youngsters each very nervous, most high as kites. Many had not left the village before, and had certainly never travelled in a car. The motion sickness vomiting began quite early and the four hours it took to reach Bandaradougou seemed like several days. Joseph was as patient as he could manage but he was a man and his desire to get the journey done constantly battled with his compassion towards a tiny queasy tummy. Eve and Joseph had one of their more difficult marital moments as she reinforced the compassionate side of his nature by threatening to kill him on one occasion, if he didn't stop. Already her maternal instincts were rising on behalf of those in her care.

Back at the church compound everybody was washed and all heads were shaved. Axelle's mother Aicha, a seamstress in the city walked over from Boulon–Bossie to measure everybody. Eve had asked her to make a pretty uniform dress for each girl. Aicha had managed to acquire a substantial bolt of lovely yellow and white checked fabric.

The girls were each equipped with tooth brushes, a roll mat to sleep on, and some soap. Very few had brought any possessions; they had nothing to bring.

Lessons were taken by Eve and Joseph, both of whom were the most educated adults in the village. Prayers for a school teacher continued. The only money they had available was what was given by the church in special offerings. All of that was needed to feed the girls and provide basic stationery. The daily routine ran from 0700 hours commencing with compulsory shower, breakfast and prayers. During the day the girls were given a little free time to talk and play but mainly were engaged in language or mathematics lessons, or learning to make and to sell baskets of a Libyan design, quite affordably exotic to the city dwellers who readily bought them in their markets.

There was a main meal at noon, which was as nutritious as the project could afford. Many of the villagers helped with the supply of ingredients and were faithful to do so whenever possible. In the evenings the girls worked on the chores necessary to run the project, did a little gardening on the plot, and gathered to pray just before bed time. Eve felt like a mother to them all and spent herself on them.

Basket making was initially quite a costly initiative to attempt but very soon began to earn the girls money. They were allowed to keep most of their earnings though encouraged to make a small contribution to the Lydia Girls Project. Eve taught Aboubacar's wife Aminata to run a little micro–enterprise system where the girls could bank their own money and build up funds to buy their own materials. They began to acquire business skills and for the first time in their lives to have a little capital.

Eve was extremely strict about product quality. She would not allow the girls to produce anything shoddy as the baskets were quite distinctive. The Libyan style was unusual and quite recognizable. Any quality failure would reflect badly on them all.

For six months or so the little vocational training school struggled along. Eve had never felt so fulfilled before. Nothing she had done had so filled her with joy and enthusiasm. The girls learned hungrily. Their lives had been free from investment until this time and they could see their own skills and abilities forming, opening up opportunities for their future that they had previously had no clue existed. Their shyness had quickly evaporated, and Eve found herself among a vibrant vocal assertive crowd of grateful reasonably respectful teenagers, an exciting place to work.

December through to March was a season in which Europeans found it possible to visit Burkina Faso. The oppressive heat, and the fact that the nation was largely free of sight seeing opportunities conspired to keep numbers comparatively low, but some European Christians came.

A couple from Denmark, Mads and Freja came to visit, while in the Bobo–Dioulasso region. They were acquaintances of a former

ICTC student who had spoken of Joseph and his little church plant to the North of Bobo. They had a small financial gift to hand over, and tracked him down via Serge the church leader who facilitated the original mission trip and hosted Joseph and Eve when they had first come down from Ouaga with Michel.

Freja was a social worker with a keen interest in social issues in the developing world, particularly female mutilation and child nutrition. She was the driving force in the expedition.

Mads was a warm and highly intelligent man, a doctor of mathematics, now the owner of a highly rated data security management business. He had rarely if ever stayed at a hotel standard below five star and was not enjoying a 10–day sojourn in the white man's graveyard, West Africa. He had never before seen sights like those he'd encountered here, and the impact of the deprivation he'd observed was making him stressed and angry.

The simple mud block cube shaped houses along the roadsides, windowless and horrible, some with no roof at all, had been an indication of what he might find when he got out into the villages with his host. Here he found children running around naked, not because it was warm and that was what they wanted, but because they had no clothes. Some of the older ones had just a football shirt, worn like a short dress, making a very poor show of providing some modest decency.

Half collapsing mud brick houses with straw roofs, no mosquito nets, no windows and barely any furniture housed swarms of people. He noted the fetishes, the thatched mud built grain huts and the disheveled fences that marked off the compounds. Each compound contained a network of huts indicative of swelling family numbers. More mouths competing for the same harvest yields. The men sat around drinking and talking. Harassed looking women struggled with inadequate tools to attend to the needs of their men and children who ran barefoot everywhere, clambering over walls and peeking through doorways, giggling when they saw he noticed them.

He had been offered dolo — the millet beer quaffed by the villagers. His host had warned him not to drink this for two reasons: for one, Christians should not drink alcohol; and two, his system simply wouldn't have the antibodies necessary to protect him and it seemed a long way to come just to die. He had heeded the warning.

He could see no reason why such abject poverty could be allowed to continue. There was no health provision in most villages, few schools, awful water arrangements with no attention paid to hygiene. He had observed open untreated ulcerated wounds, malnourished children, very thin people in ragged clothing and open fires heating uninteresting looking vegetarian food in battered pots propped up on large stones.

For Mads much of this could have been sorted out with a bit of reorganization and some targeted focused resources through good local leadership. He could not see the vast web of spiritual, educational, tribal and prejudicial issues which together contributed to the mess. To him everything was easy to solve and someone just needed to get a grip and sort it all out.

Joseph was delighted to meet Mads and Freja. They were his first European visitors, arriving late in the afternoon one Wednesday. They both spoke French which was helpful as Eve's English was barely functional. As they shook hands Joseph was reminded that Europeans smelled of chemicals. He refrained from wrinkling his nose. Eve had killed a chicken and gathered some herbs, preparing rice and going to a lot of trouble serving her finest menu on the scruffy tin plates which she had scrubbed thoroughly with well water. They had no cutlery.

Freja, perched on a crudely made bench, slightly concerned about splinters where she least wanted them, visibly quailed at the sight of the food. She didn't like the idea of putting her fingers into the steaming hot casserole–like mixture. Joseph smiled, reading her body language and recalled the problems he had needed to overcome when using cutlery at first. He had kept burning his mouth because his normal way of testing food temperature was with his fingers. She was worried about burning her fingers. He said nothing but watched carefully, silently amused though considerate. It was very good of her to come and visit him. He was human though and some things were unavoidably funny to watch.

Joseph was very sure that his wife's hygiene standards were high enough to safely feed these Europeans. He had been trained by McDonald's after all. Eve was concerned that she make her guests feel special, particularly Freja, and mortified that the best she could do with food did not seem to be good enough for her visitor.

Mads was hungry and was able to eat his food, though with some difficulty, carefully watching how Joseph ate. When he realized that Eve was not going to sit down with them, he insisted that she did so. This was a source of embarrassment to Joseph who was so used to being served, especially when hosting guests; that he had not previously picked up that others may detect a hint of misogyny. His behaviour was absolutely normal in his culture and Eve was more than happy to serve everyone; preferring to do that to a high standard than to join them at the table. Mads thought he was honouring Eve and demonstrating his culture's superior approach to women so that Joseph could learn from his excellent example. In fact he confused and irritated them both, though they remained charming.

After the meal they drank tea. Joseph was aware that Europeans liked their tea hot and strong, but the dynamics of such a preparation in Bandaradougou were not easy to arrange. At ICTC tea was made by simply switching on an electric kettle. Here sticks had to be collected, a fire lit, a pot boiled and then the tea brewed. Keeping the pot free from ash was difficult, and often the tea was cloudy and usually there was not enough time so the water was not hot enough. By the time it reached the drinker, it was fairly unpalatable. Freja did not drink hers. She had a bottle of water from which she sipped throughout the visit.

After the tea was downed or left, their guests were shown the church. They tried to look impressed at the very basic building. In Joseph's eyes it was a wonderful gift from God, a marvelous provision and perfect for his ministry. Mads didn't like the bathroom facilities, which he visited but did not use. He decided he could wait; he'd rather use a bush.

Freja was very interested to hear about the new Lydia Girls project so they were taken over to the little classroom. Mads asked what the arrangements were. He listened with growing concern.

'…and they eat, sleep and work in this little room?'

'Yes it has been built especially for the purpose. We hope eventually to have maybe thirty girls.'

'They sit on the floor, in the mud?'

'We hope to be able to get some benches. It is difficult to do everything at once. We have started with what is in our hands.'

'They have just a bucket shower and one WC?'

'It is what we all have.'

'Their food is the same every day? They eat no meat?'

'We feed them mango and papaya and millet and rice. Also, vegetables from the land of one of our families. Sometimes we are able to get fish, and we have goat milk for them.'

'Have you done work like this before?'

'No, it is new, we are learning how to do this and have very little experience. We do not have much to share with them, but we share what we can.'

'Well then why have you taken them from their families? You feed them little, you keep them in one room, you make them eat sleep and work on the floor. They produce bags for you to trade, They are kept here like animals. I am very worried that what you are doing is going to cause them great harm.'

The meeting was not at all what Joseph was expecting. He naturally was looking for encouragement. He had thought this Danish person would be impressed with what they had achieved and how they had sacrificed all they had to help these poor girls. The man seemed angry.

'I am sorry that you do not like what we are doing. I think perhaps you have misunderstood where these girls came from. Certainly if they were European girls this would not be good for them; but here, this is a very positive thing.'

'I think you may be guilty of abusing them. These conditions are truly shocking, and they have no way of contacting their families, no way of making a complaint. They are prisoners here.'

Mads was dumping the internalized anger of his traumatic day onto Joseph. In fairness he was not himself. He was tired, emotional, culture shocked. He could and should have been more careful. He had offended Joseph. Worse he had discouraged him. That was not why he was here. He was quite relieved therefore when Joseph responded mildly and wisely.

'Perhaps we should explain more fully. Eve will tell you her story and why we have this vision.'

Mads responded positively, given a second chance. Recalling that God had given him no peace in recent months nudging his attention firmly towards Burkina Faso he remained deeply concerned and wanted to get a grasp of what was happening. He had come to Africa to help not to hinder, he readily agreed to hear the story just in case there could possibly be a reason for this appalling situation. He encouraged Eve to take her time.

Eve went right back to the beginning, starting with a description of life in Ibrahim's compound, sketching out the cruel reality of life on the margins of survival. By the time she came to mentioning her agreement with God, Freja had started to cry. Long before she finished her summary of a development and wealth comparison between villages here near the city, and those out near the border, Mads had tears in his eyes too. The Danes where most interested in the way these villagers had prioritized the girls over their own children, because they believed that was what God wanted.

The account had taught him something absolutely transformational. Somehow this highly intelligent mature Danish business leader, with all the answers and an opinion to offer on everything he saw, had learned something radical about authentic decision making and listening to God, from a young Burkinabe pastor.

Something broke in the adventurous little couple far from their chilly home. They had at first done their best to define how not to visit a courageous poverty stricken church. Taking the time to listen more carefully they could now see what ignorance they had shown. Freja promised they would return the following day. They would bring the matter before God, sleeping on it would help them think straighter she hoped. Then they were gone, back to Bobo, leaving only a cloud of dust from Serge's vehicle.

Eve and Joseph prayed together for Mads and Freja, hoping that they may be able to persuade them to accept that what they were doing here had merit. Eve was baffled by the couple's behaviour, though Joseph had a better perspective, having worked and lived among Europeans.

The following morning Mads and Freja began with an apology.

'I was foolish and disrespectful to you yesterday,' began Mads, 'please forgive me.'

Joseph was much quicker to extend forgiveness than he was to take offence. He made it clear that any small offence caused was partly his own fault; he had failed to communicate things in the right way and though there was no need for Mads to offer it, the apology was gladly accepted.

Mads and Freja explained that both had undergone great anxiety overnight. They had been challenged by the way they had viewed the girls from their perspective without once imagining the cycle of desperation and hopelessness from which they were being rescued. Freja had dreamed a dream which she believed had come from God. It was one of a child born in desperate need of professional medical support. The child had not lived. There was much detail concerning her role as a doctor and of Mads who was there in some administrative capacity, too busy to direct resource to the baby in time.

The couple promised nothing except the seriousness of their commitment. They asked of Joseph how much money it cost to keep the girls. The response was a little over 10 Krone per week, approximately one and a half US dollars.

Before they left, as a down payment on their commitment they handed Joseph $1500 US. It was their emergency cash in case they got into problems beyond the reach of Mastercard. They would take their chances.

11. REGRETS

Rick and Pamela made a lot of time available to Candice. She loved the fortnightly meetings she and Pamela set up to work through the implications of her radical discipleship. She spent Wednesday afternoon with Pamela, the evening with the family, though mostly all three kids were away in college.

For one thing Pamela was an incredible cook, with a lot of experience of South Asian food. She had an intimate understanding of exotic ingredients: fish sauce, lemon grass, Vietnamese coriander, holy basil, bird's eye chili, and many more which Candice had not previously encountered. She was not just knowledgeable, she would conjure healthy aromatic dishes of incredible freshness and bursting flavours that Candice relished and consumed with joy.

It was not just food; she taught Candice to roast coffee beans in a wok, and how to produce the most incredible iced coffee and unbelievable tropical fruit smoothies.

Somehow whenever she visited them, Candice felt like she had spent a little time with Tolkien's elves at Rivendell. She always came away feeling fantastic. Rick would say something like, 'Candice, you're a good girl.' and she would feel ten foot tall. It wasn't the words, it was the tone.

Her own dad had left the family home when she had been twelve years old. Candice partly blamed herself for the break–up. Her dad had complained many times that she was in the way or had messed the house up, was costing him a packet what with gym classes and uniforms and school and stuff. He had become increasingly miserable around the house for a couple of years and he and her mom had been openly hostile. Candice had felt part of something that he didn't want. He'd bought her the Jeep and had sometimes come to watch her at football games but he made little attempt to see her on her own. She really had no idea how she felt about her, he certainly hadn't taken a great deal of interest in her. He'd moved on.

With Rick there was always something to talk about. She noticed he was careful never to be alone with her and she only really knew him as 'Rick and Pamela' which was a helpful and relaxing dynamic. She loved to get him talking about his life's work. This was when he was most animated. Living in the USA was the consequence of placing his own children above his ministry: 'If we can't nurture our own kids properly, what have we got to offer anyone else's?'

He had been running a programme in the slum on the edge of Phúc Xá Ward in the Ba Dình District of Hà Nôi, Vietnam's beautiful green second city far to the North of the capital Ho Chi Minh City.

One evening, after Candice had enjoyed a delicious meal of sticky rice and fish sauce wings, he described how the programme had begun.

'I took an agricultural qualification after seminary, planning to help the farmers out a little with some kind of training input, maybe setting up an NGO or something. My dad had done something similar with the Thai Karen.

'Anyways we arrived out in Hà Nôi and were doing our acclimatization, settling in, trying to figure out what next. I recall taking an interest in Phúc Xá down near the fruit market. There was a whole bunch of people living there, farmers who'd moved into the city mostly. They were working in the markets, understood fruit and vegetables and had contacts in the villages. Also there were some folks in the slum that recycled scrap and stuff. Most of the houses were informal shacks and the people paid maybe 30 or 40 dollars per month to be there.

'I used to go down by the river a bit, and got kinda used to seeing a kid of maybe four or five years old begging with a tin. We had been advised by the mission agency not to give any money to beggars as they would be likely to spend the money on drugs or alcohol. I would use a few dông and buy him some food though. It was difficult not to and he was such a sweet kid. He and I started speaking and I learned his name, Minh.

'One night I was riding my scooter down there by the river quite late, maybe 11 p.m. or so and I noticed Minh sat begging with his tin. I stopped and asked why he was out so late. He said he'd been forced to sit there and beg. I asked who forced him and he said a gang of older boys.

'Turned out he was homeless, mum had died or something, no dad. This gang had picked him up and was using him to beg for them. They said if he didn't they would cut him up and throw him in the river. He had seen them do this to another kid. He was awake so late because they had been giving him amphetamines.

'Didn't seem like there was much I could do so I got on my bike and rode back to our little apartment, shut myself in our bedroom. I just cried and cried to God that such things should happen to children. That he could let such things happen.

'I tell you, Candice, I have never heard the audible voice of God. Some people tell me they have, but it hasn't happened *for me. What happened that night was something else, like a thought planted in my head. Felt like an idea of my own, you know, like a brainwave or something, but more conversational. Went something like: "I am not letting this happen, you are."*

'*That busted me up a bit. I felt like justifying myself with things like the advice the mission agency had given us, the need to keep a low profile and avoid anything that drew attention to ourselves. We were on visas that could get ripped up any time and we could have found ourselves on a plane home, mission career over just like that. Kind of gets to you; eats away at your confidence. There weren't any excuses actually, I had failed that kid and I knew it.*

'*I spoke with Pamela and we prayed together. There was only one thing I could do. Kinda felt like I had a mandate from God that overrode everything else. I got back on my bike, rode around there and picked the kid up, took him to where his gang hung out and told those boys he was coming with me; then I rode home with him.*'

Pamela chipped in, 'I was horrified when he first told me what he was thinking of but as Rick explained what had happened with him and God and all and we prayed it over there was an unusual amount of peace in my spirit about the risks. I guess I just accepted that things would be a bit crazy for a few days. That turned into four months, until we found a family from the church willing to take him in if we covered his expenses.'

Rick was eager to take the story on again. He was on a roll, eyes shining; full of excitement as memories of events that had shaped their lives tumbled out of him.

'*From then on it was all about street kids. We forgot about agriculture and stuff, and began to look for ways of working with these little ones. We had to switch mission agencies as our focus shifted to the slum and the kids who lived around there. We got passed on to a brilliant outfit that gave us some great advice and really came through with support, kept encouraging and visiting and everything. Rick got some peer mentoring from a group over in Chiang Mai.*

'We rented an old shack near the market, ran some lessons in there; began feeding the kids. The new mission agency put some support in and we found we were able to bathe them, clothe them, feed them; get them some education. Occasionally when there was a serious health issue we'd take them to a hospital and fund their treatment. I suppose we just poured our lives into that little slum from then on.

'We got some incredible help from some folks in Malaysia who came down to see what we were doing. They built us a wonderful facility with a basketball court and all. We were able to take on some local staff we picked up in the state church we attended. Having them around enabled us to share our life and ministry with them. They're running it all now, we just meet with them weekly over Skype; keep a handle on how they're going.

'It was pretty tough on us and the kids in the early days. We never could afford a car or anything. When you're surrounded by needs like that, you just have to keep pouring in what you can. I got hold of this motorbike and sidecar.'

Pamela added, 'It was really dangerous, their traffic is a nightmare for westerners, and the big vehicles, trucks and buses just barge you out of the way. We had three small children. Two used to ride with me in the sidecar, our oldest in front of Rick on the saddle.'

Rick was back on the narrative:

'The best part about those days for me was we had some of those boys from the gang that abused Minh join the programme pretty early on. One of them became a staffer eventually, although he's struggled a little with his family putting pressure on him to get back into drugs and gambling and stuff.'

Candice was a little tearful as she listened to this gritty couple share their journey with her. 'How much of yourselves have you left back there in Vietnam?'

'Pretty much all of us, I'd say,' Rick responded. Pamela nodded tearfully. Serving their own kids was costing them emotionally.

'Take me back with you when you return!'

'Can't do that Candice, you cannot travel our journey. You have your own journey to walk and it's only just starting. You're a good girl Candice. God has some big plans for you.'

As usual Candice left their place feeling like she'd won a million dollars. These informal get together times with Pamela followed by a meal with them both were shaping her life. She was getting the stretch she'd asked Ellen for and was grateful to the church for helping her respond to what had happened on the mission trip last year.

Candice took a job waitressing at a little Thai place down in Old Town. It was a long way from sports science but she did very well in tips. She wanted to get a feel for South Asian culture, to experience working with and for Thai people.

Taking the job allowed her to give her mother some money and take some time to work out what she would do with her future. Rick and Pamela had advised that she should take a course at somewhere outstanding like Eastern or Azusa in preparation for effective overseas service.

She sold the Jeep, bought an ageing Diesel Golf, which was extremely inexpensive to buy and cut her gas budget by two thirds. She started saving hard for her course costs, and began the process of application for post graduate mission courses.

• • •

Working out what he would do with his future was also occupying Casper's restless mind. His portfolio of projects was overflowing and the relentless demands on his time cutting into his social life to the extent that he didn't have one. Maintaining his golden boy image was becoming trickier as the demands of his investors piled the pressure on. He still had no doubt that he could deliver most projects but it was nowhere near as straightforward as he had expected. He steered away from all things medical and genetic in order to avoid endless testing and battles with ethical lobbyists. He smiled as he recalled a proposal that he'd shredded involving crossing spiders with cows in order to create enormous glands that produced commercially viable quantities of spider web. The bidder certainly claimed to be able to come up with the strongest fibre available, but not the strongest proposal.

His preference was for high end technology: weapons systems, devices for luxury homes and yachts, and cool stuff that could become fashionable. He was looking seriously at a proposal for defending warships involving creating a web of thin but very strong netting delivered by enormous starburst firework–like rockets into the sector from which incoming ordinance was detected. The netting would collect then explode incoming missiles. It looked feasible, much more reliable perhaps than trying to hit incoming weapons with ship based anti missile missiles. Ships were pricey things and with his dad in the procurement department he could combine an inside track, a vast budget and a viable option — tasty! The tricky part was going to be getting enough webbing up there fast enough, strong enough and spread wide enough. Maybe he shouldn't have shredded that crazy spider web and cow genetics paper! He grinned, mostly he loved this job.

He could sustain his current pace for another couple of years then he planned to move on to something a little more morally rewarding. He had listened to a recording of some 'big shot'; preaching about how what we did for a living needed to be about more than paying the bills and funding our lifestyles. His mouth formed a wry smile as he imagined what Candice would say if she knew he had on reflection re–run her cutting words regarding values over and again since their bruising final date.

He had observed Candice spending a lot of time with Rick and Pamela. She clearly rated them highly and he had noticed that whatever they did in connection with church life was always done to the highest standards. He decided they might be a good port of call for a conversation about what he might do with his life after a few more years of building up security.

'Sure, come around and see us any evening except Wednesdays. Give us a call first and we'll deal you in for dinner.' Rick could not have been more approachable.

The call duly made, Casper's shiny patent leather Italian shoes appeared on the Harris's doorstep the following Thursday evening. The food was exquisite and he being an impressive eater, she a wonderful chef, Casper and Pamela hit it off very well. Rick was charming and affable. He enquired what Casper did for a living, and tried to stay with the response.

'Wow! You keep busy young man. Not sure I have the brains to cope with what you said there. Drones and stuff researchers, developers, manufacturers, marketing people and investors. You have a lot to keep in balance.' He looked concerned rather than impressed.

Casper was anxious to get around to the reason why he called and explained that he was thinking beyond this phase of his life. Looking further into the future he wanted to put some energy into volunteering or appropriate technology or something. He'd heard that they were familiar with the missionary scene, might have a few contacts they could pass over, strings they could pull to introduce him to the right people.

Rick was the first to offer some suggestions. 'Well, young man, you're heading in a fine direction there, but maybe we need to back up a little bit and ask some questions about why you might be thinking this way.'

Casper gave his reasons, carefully excluding any mention of Candice. He did his best to present a good show to these people. They were after all people of God. He wanted to look his best in their eyes.

He was not aware that they knew all about Candice, and actually he was cruelly exposed here. They knew about the separate cars and the values mismatch. He could not have come to a better place, he was in good hands. These two knew something about grace and forgiveness. It was the language and currency of their ministry. They also knew what to do with half truth and deceit.

Pamela smiled and assured him that God was very interested in bringing about a change in direction for people; in fact she had been involved in facilitating quite a few career changes over the years. She decided to give him the inside track on some of that.

She explained that she had begun her training for working with those affected by the deepest ravages of poverty, with a little ministry based in the night markets over in Ho Chi Minh. Here the bar girls plied their trade, often accompanied by their tiny children, the product of their activities. The kids were called flower children, and were firmly anchored to the 'at risk' end of the at risk register. Left unaccompanied in the bars, selling flowers while mum entertained clients, the children were often subject to horrifying abuse, sometimes with the well compensated collusion of their mother.

The team which trained Pamela looked at the situation, trying to get God's perspective on it. He loved these girls and their customers. He loved their children too. What would he do to bring change to this situation?

The team decided to ask the girls if there was anything they could do to help them be better prostitutes. The girls asked for language lessons and child care. The team facilitated both, with the outcome that the girls were freer to work without having to look out for their children and could trade more effectively with Western customers, many of whom spoke English, very few spoke Vietnamese. The children of course loved learning about God, had a great time and stopped working the bars.

After a time there was sufficient trust and relationship to ask questions such as: 'Is this the occupation you'd most like to do to earn money?'

They explained that they were development specialists thinking of launching a high quality café and wanted to train local cooks, administrators and service personnel to run it: 'Eventually we want to be able to transfer full ownership to the team which is hands–on running the venture. Would something like that interest you?'

Casper was impressed. 'Whoa! So you actually got right behind these people — even though you disagreed with what they were doing?'

'The project was training me, I was a learner there. Yes they did.'

Casper noted she had deflected any credit away from herself. A trustworthy person, he mused.

'Why did you tell me about it?'

> 'I wanted to show you that when God brings about a change in direction, he does so in a non–judgmental way. The team in Ho Chi Minh picked up that it wasn't too much of an issue to him what these girls were doing, it mattered to him who they were and what they could be doing.

> 'There are two things to think about there. Firstly, if you are going to do things with God you must have a dynamic relationship with him. There is no way the Ho Chi Minh team could have figured out God's strategy for the girls without knowing him and picking up how he felt about them. For that to happen you have to have something real going on between you and God. Secondly, you have to realize that the team was merely reflecting the way God wanted to act. They were obedient to him, and therefore got to participate in what he is like. I guess what happened indicates that, however you feel about yourself. What you're into that he might not approve of isn't a huge problem for God to sort

out. He can get you out there as soon as you want to let go of whatever it is that's wrecking your life.'

Casper sat weighing these words, feeling the love and wisdom of an old warrior whose weapons were love, reconciliation and forgiveness. It was a window on a different world to his — a kingdom if you like, steadily growing as it untangled the mess made by human choices. It saw individuals as valuable and set them free from their past, giving them hope and a future. It was a context for extraordinarily positive actions which could value and honour those in need, and confront and disarm those who were into exploiting others. Casper's world was one of gaining an edge. He was a master at furthering his own interests, often at the expense of others. He didn't really fit into Pamela's world at all. He thought he might like to.

There were some matters in his private world that he simply could not discuss here. He was still utterly fascinated with lurid images and had completely lost control of his sexual conduct. He still indulged in high risk gambling, still backed the companies ransacking Africa's fertile soil, though he was beginning to comprehend what this might be doing to the indigenous people. He had the detailed statistics on what was happening, his personal fortune depended on his knowledge of them.

He had started drinking fairly heavily in the late evenings now. With his very high pressure of work, love life and addictions, there was absolutely no space or time for any genuine communication to happen between himself and God.

Just before he left the house Casper nearly came to the point of bringing up the subject of his secret world. He felt this was a place where it might be possible to do that, to get some help. He just could not cope with the shame, and retreated from the brink of a confessional moment.

He thanked Rick and Pamela, returning home with his mind a whirl of conflicting emotions. He had seen a chink of light in an otherwise increasingly dark inner world. He bitterly regretted not taking his chance in the moment of encountering something almost tangible of God in Rick and Pamela.

On the same Sunday after church, Casper, along with the other members of the Ablaze leadership team was invited to lunch at Casa de Pico over at La Mesa. He was the only volunteer present, invited mainly because they would have paid him for his role fronting the worship band if he'd needed it, and everybody liked him. He was good to be around, with razor sharp wit, dazzling smile, designer clothes and the presence of a movie star. The food was absolutely incredible, and you could bathe a small hippo in their large marguerites.

The meeting that morning had been especially good. The worship outstanding as usual and Garry had fired them all up with a rousing presentation on mission with a view to mobilizing high numbers for the following summer's programme.

The meal was a celebration. The church had hit all its numbers for the quarter, and Garry always threw a party when that happened. The laughter flowed around the table. Here was a company of people at ease with one another. Their jobs were secure, their ministry was successful; a solid high performing team.

Ellen sat next to Casper. She was pleased to see his eyes drawn towards her delightful cleavage and made sure to lean across him a few times during the meal. When he was quick with a cheeky remark as the conversation crackled and sparked with the humour of friendships, she pinched his hip playfully. She made sure that the slit in her skirt gave him an excellent view of her lovely smooth legs. When he brushed a hand against her thigh, testing, wondering, her eyes met his, welcoming, dangerously inviting. He was titillated, the more interested because the fruit was forbidden.

Ellen was past the point of caring. She had decided on her exit strategy from ministry. She had at first hinted, then stated, then insisted that Garry get her out of the trap he'd gotten them into. She hated the church, hated her role in the dreadful suffocating cameo she was forced to play. She could not, would not continue to play it. He had not heard her. Nothing stood in the way of his mission, the dream he was building, the team he was investing in, the goals they were going for.

She had considered her options, and now she was reaching for the ministry suicide pill. An affair with a highly attractive sexually exciting co-leader was exactly the exit she needed. There would be no coming back from that. It might destroy Garry's ministry; if so, good! His ministry was her rival.

After the meal Casper spent the evening alone on the Point Loma beach boardwalk, watching the pelicans glide lazily by until the gloom of dusk changed his focus from living things to twinkling lights and reflections of moonlight. As the surf pounded the sand and the powerful wash of the sounds of wind and wave laid down a deafening yet soothing sound track to his thoughts he worked through his options.

He returned to his exquisite apartment at 10 p.m. and reached for the phone, a woman's voice answered and softened when she recognized him. 'Oh hi Casper, it's quite late, are you OK?'

12. BURNING BRIDGES

Mads and Freja returned to Copenhagen, heads filled with disturbing images of real life, hearts broken.

They had left Europe for a whistle stop tour of Mali, South Sudan and Burkina Faso, under the impression that the world was blessed with systems and governance that were basically good. They thought that while needing some improvements it was generally as just and fair as could be managed. The UN, Médecins Sans Frontières, UNESCO, Amnesty International, the Red Cross and many other pan–world alliances and agencies were delivering as much justice as was practically possible. Their view was that induced by Hollywood. For the anarchy and chaos of Mad Max's world to become reality there would have to be a total collapse of the existing systems.

They returned to their home in Glostrup, Copenhagen with their eyes opened by the first hand accounts of the displaced or traumatized people they had met and the sights they had witnessed.

For a vast number of men women and children in sub–Saharan Africa particularly in Sudan, parts of Mali, Somalia, Sierra Leone, Ethiopia and Eritrea, there was no workable system of justice. Small governments were dedicated primarily to holding on to power, ignoring the plight of people needlessly dying. There were armed groups mercilessly oppressing the helpless. Whole regions were in the grip of cruel unaccountable brigands. Local despots, often using religious rhetoric to justify horrendous criminal behaviour, brought misery and constant fear to millions of people.

Mads and Freja had glimpsed shards of hope piercing the poverty and despair. None more so than the brave efforts being made in Bandaradougou to address the needs of girls; which they had so misjudged. They had been quick to assume that Eve's little team had failed to share enough of their resource to provide adequately for the girls. The truth was, they had given up to and beyond their means at the expense of their own ends.

Mads and Freja spent a little time with their minister and a couple of trusted friends, explaining what had happened. They continued to have no peace about their priorities and where they were directing their energies. Mads, ever the decisive man of action, suggested that they downsize their home, and use the equity on their property to finance construction of decent facilities in Bandaradougou.

Within six months he was back in Serge's car, pulling up outside Joseph and Eve's compound. He was pleased to notice when he looked in at the little classroom that there were now some crude desk benches, on which sat 20 young girls. Eve was obviously using the money, specifically on the project to which it had been given. There was much discussion involving architects, planning permission, builders and electricity supplies. Budgets were drawn up and a significant building approved, costed and commissioned. It would provide decent living and sleeping accommodation for 80 girls, including a kitchen, bathrooms and spacious classrooms. Mads insisted on ensuring that foundations were dug that could support more floors in the future if necessary.

Eve and Joseph sat with Mads and discussed a sponsorship programme. They agreed that it would not be practical for them to arrange individual communication between sponsored children and their donors. They wanted to have a more fluid system which allowed them to report total figures and total numbers in the programme, whereby donors could easily check on the efficient use of funds. They also wanted to be free of one of the headaches some of the agencies, now known to Joseph, confided to him. This occurred when a donor dropped out leaving a sponsored child abandoned.

Mads made a reconnaissance of potential local industry that would allow him to arrange for export trade, bringing some much needed wealth to the area. There was however, very little that would be of interest to his European friends. He left with some half formed thoughts about dried fruits and ground nuts. He also took back a list of technological needs such as solar panels for electricity, water pumps for irrigation and canning and packaging machinery. He was concerned though that his ideas should not compromise the villagers' own needs. It would be a delicate balance to strike, and one which would demand detailed dialogue with the local leaders considering implications.

Mads found himself increasingly consumed with helping Eve's project in particular. He was less interested now in the development of software for European markets and he began the process of handing on the daily leadership of his company to his close friend and co-founder Mikkel. They agreed that Mads could step out of the business and receive a small ongoing share of nett profits to be reviewed annually indefinitely. Mads agreed to operate as a sleeping minority partner; consulting on development for as long as his knowledge of their field remained current. This was likely to be less than three years.

Eve needed something more for the girls. It was not enough for them to graduate from her programme just as basket makers.

Sponsorship coming through Mads had been upgraded. Primarily because his budgeting skills had helped them to include everything the girls needed for their development path to be successful. There was now a more than sufficient flow of funds to pay for teachers to come out from the city three times per week. On subsequent days the girls were taught mathematics, Mòoré and French. The teachers were able to teach to accredited standards, something Eve could not do. She could however look at their books — something she did often. Picking up Djènèba's book at the end of the first year her eyes had welled with tears of delight as she observed page after page of neat writing, each page bearing the mark 10/10 from the teacher.

Djènèba had been one of the first girls to come from Djigouera and whose first lessons in mathematics had been taken by Eve. Without Lydia Girls, Djènèba would have been illiterate, innumerate, and may by now have been carrying one of many children in a family living in and bound for grinding poverty.

It was a church group from England, one which included a slightly pie–eyed Giles (his room mate from ICTC) that made the most significant breakthrough in vocational training.

After the initial greetings which included a couple of rituals:

'Are you tired?'

'Yes'

'Do you want some supper?'

'No'

They both roared with laughter at the recollection of their first meeting.

'Let me pray for you.'

'Thank you.'

> *'God is gonna increase you, he is gonna pour goodness upon you, he is gonna rain down blessing on your finances, on your family, on your home, on your body, he is gonna make you stronger.....'*

The affected strong Italian accent trailed away drowned in a howl of laughter from them both. It was good to be together again.

Giles's little team brought a bit of financial help, did some preaching with them, showed them how to use a video projector and video player. Giles's practical skills came to the fore in setting up and running a little generator for the purpose.

Joseph took Giles and some of his own leaders to run a little mission trip to a village ten miles further out from the city. The village chief had been asking them to send him a pastor, he wanted a church. Some of his relatives were in Boulon–Bossie. He had heard great things about the church in Bandaradougou; in fact he was one of those who had sent Eve a body to raise from the dead. His sister Oumou and brother–in–law Salif were church members. Oumou's account of the changes in their marriage, particularly Salif's behaviour towards her and the children and the way he spent money had pleased and intrigued the chief. He thought a church might be good for his village.

Joseph greeted the chief, thanking him for the invitation and introducing Giles and his team. The chief was very pleased indeed to be introduced to Europeans. He rolled out the millet beer and saghbo, the first of which was declined, the second picked at gamely. Giles was especially attentive to giving thanks for this food on this occasion.

They asked if it would be possible to video the chief telling the story of the village, something he was very eager to do.

That evening after the sun set, they showed the chief and his story on the big screen. They then showed the Jesus video, which had been translated into Djula. Giles watched fascinated as the villagers cried openly at the scene of Christ's execution, and clapped and cheered noisily when he was raised from the dead. Joseph preached, there was a significant response.

They left the village's new congregation in the hands of Salif and Oumou who had agreed to stay on for a few weeks, promising to contact the Bible College at Ouaga and arrange for a young pastor to be sent there as soon as possible to begin the process of constructing a church and possibly a building with help from the denominational HQ.

On the last evening of his visit, Joseph, Eve and Giles were up late into the night discussing the future of the Lydia Girls programme. Giles suggested they look at teaching the girls to sew. Eve was excited about this and knew a couple of people who could maybe help. There was certainly room for a seamstress in every village. If they could equip the girls with this skill, they would have a way of providing for their families beyond the subsistence farming which was the norm.

Eve and Joseph set aside the money brought by Giles and his team for a couple of sewing machines and some fabric.

Aicha from Boulon–Bossie came over and helped out with purchasing fabric, and basic instructions. She was skilled as a seamstress, but limited as a teacher. Some instruction was possible, but it would be difficult to get the girls to a commercial standard without proper training. Aicha, whose work in the city was in making garments, found someone capable and willing to teach.

On his next visit Mads found himself reworking the budget and sponsorship arrangements to include training in seamstress skills, a sewing machine as a leaving gift, and a supply of fabric to each girl for initial training. Once their skills were honed sufficiently to take on commercial work, towards the end of their training the girls could add their earnings from garment making to those of selling bags.

The new building was opened in March of the following year, and with the growing reputation of Lydia Girls spreading far and wide, recruitment was very straightforward. From now on they would be able to take as many girls as sponsorship would allow.

Mads had built a Danish nonprofit organization specifically in support of Lydia Girls. He was doing the church circuit in Denmark and was hoping to expand his reach into Sweden and Norway. He had built a website which kept donors informed with detailed and helpful reports on how the Lydia Girls project was progressing.

Joseph became much less directly involved in Lydia Girls after two or three years of its existence. It was very much Eve's project. At the end of the third year when the first eight girls returned to Djigouera, there were tears of both joy and sadness. Eight young women, straight backed, strong, well nourished, beautiful, educated and well dressed climbed out of the Isuzu. They were simply unrecognizable from the girls that had left the village; each one, with her own means, with business savvy, and with a sewing machine, was ready to begin a new way of life.

Florence and Eve stared into one another's eyes. Florence's kindness and personal investment towards Eve many years previously had led to this moment when eight beautiful capable women rejoined her village and joined her church.

The girls planned to initially work together producing garments as one collective, but then to split up and make their way to the city and to other villages to ply their trade. For them there was no looking back. If you wanted to add one of these girls to your compound of wives and children, you could forget it. They were aiming higher.

13. CONFERRING

A hush fell on the auditorium, the lights burned and the speaker's face shone with perspiration. This was the final plenary session of what had been an excellent conference.

> '"I confer on you a Kingdom and you will eat with me and drink with me and sit on thrones," he read.

His voice sounded like he might have been South African. It was a weird accent, like someone who'd lived in so many places he'd all but lost touch with the culture he started out with.

> 'These words are found in the mouth of Jesus in the New Testament. They are trustworthy words, spoken over a meal by the Creator to his friends. The following day he would die at the hands of the empire to which he had given the temporary authority to rule his world and at the behest of leaders from whom he had just removed the spiritual authority to guide.

'The words were preceded by some of the most extraordinary descriptions of authentic leadership ever recorded, known globally, but rarely in my experience adequately followed.'

Candice sat rapt, down near the front, wearing her steward's vest, staring up at her professor. She had made it to Pacific for a Masters in Transformational Leadership. She was home following a placement with Rick's people in Phúc Xá. Her mind was filled with the whirl of experiences to which the last seven months had exposed her: the smells and the sounds of the fruit market, voices shouting, stall holders cooking and eating at their stalls, children sat silently staring as the endless crowds jostled past; learning to cross a road where there is never a gap in traffic, never a safe moment to step out, flinching as the vehicles and bicycles wash around you as you try to hold a steady course through the chaos.

Candice's Vietnamese was progressing steadily. She could get by on her own in the market now, and has just starting to be able to interact with her neighbours. She was staying with a dear little family in the slum. Her bed just five foot six long filled most of the space and left her barely enough room to dress in the tiny bedroom. She was safe there, valued and cared for among the desperate and the needy. Starting to feel like one of them, learning how to live with nothing. She had taken a few things with her: favourite clothes, a couple of old comforts but they had been stolen outside the airport by a thief on a moped. At first she had wept tears of anger and frustration. Where was God in that? She had later learnt to give thanks for the lesson of empathy she had received. Another tie with her wealth and her past had been cut, another step towards authenticity. She was becoming more fit to serve the poor.

It was Rick and Pamela who suggested this course. They believed most strongly that the course leader walked the walk. They had suggested that she gain an education before visiting her actions on the world's poor. They couldn't recommend the speaker more highly. There were other great friends of the poor, but this fellow was their friend too.

Candice had a long way to travel yet before she could be alongside the children she wanted to care for, to reach, love. She was on her way though, and one day, one day soon, she was sure she would be able to serve them. Rick was right, this was her journey, and her King was becoming more distinct in the mist as she drew closer to him and to those he called her to serve for him.

She was happy being single. She loved children and bearing children was a joy she had explored in her fantasy world since she was a little girl. She was now aware though of the countless children with no mom to love them. She had found something more important to her than her instincts.

The words of the speaker drew her back to the auditorium:

> '"The kings of pagan nations Lord it over them, and those who exercise authority over them say they are their benefactors." By this he was describing those who through their contrivance had made it to the top of the heap and he was observing that they very much liked to push people around. At the same time they would make a convincing show of saying that their leadership was a good thing for those whose butts they kicked.

> 'Now Jesus, more than likely a construction worker on some of those big old projects Herod Antipas was running, would have known all about being pushed around. He'd also have known what kind of social behaviour the rulers exhibited. His cousin had been beheaded at a party thrown by one of them.

> 'The abuse of power is the natural result of leaders whose values are self-seeking, whose hearts are not being reworked by the Spirit of God. Their power structures are temporary, granted by the Creator because he, the ultimate sociologist, knows that even a tyrant's rule is better than no rule at all. The kind of behaviour he attributes to rulers of the pagan nations doesn't wash in the permanent Kingdom; the Kingdom of God. He makes this very clear: "But you are not to be like that. Instead, the greatest among you should be like the youngest, and the one who rules like the one who serves."'

Casper was listening very intently too. He was sat near the back. It had been Rick's suggestion that he attend the conference. Things had been a little different since that Sunday night when he'd called up Pamela. She had suggested he come straight over and meet with them and talk out what was troubling him.

There in the Harris home he'd talked through what was really going on in his private little world. He talked about the dawning implications of being party to messing with the price of food. He confessed to the promiscuity, the concealment of his private life to protect his ministry façade. He spoke of his addiction to porn and desperation that he could never ever get close to anyone with all this sneaking around going on. And he cried, not tears of self–pity, tears of desperation, of regret, of despair.

He confessed to how close he had come to starting an affair with the minister's wife, a trusted friend, someone he admired. He had reached the point where the fun had ceased. In a life where it was his birthday every day, he longed for truth and meaning and eternal significance.

He'd come to the right place. Rick and Pamela explained that God had no issues with confessed crap. That could all be skimmed off and cleaned up easily enough. There were all sorts of examples of people that Jesus had met: demoniacs, prostitutes, thieves, fraudsters and so on. His relationships with them were as individual as the people were unique. However his message was always the same: 'Change. I have something better for you, the Kingdom of God is here.'

'You want significance, my boy? You're gonna have to get some creases in those knees, maybe scuff up those shiny shoes!'

Casper had cashed in his chips with CityTradeIndex and pulled his money out of his commodity trading as soon as his futures contracts reached their delivery dates.

He had a couple of ideas about trying to use his capital to buy up some staples in the most pressurized areas and release the grains at a fair price throughout the hard months through June to

September. That way he hoped to smack those unscrupulous pitiless traders who literally starved the poor into paying whatever they asked for their stockpiled food. He was just looking for a smart decent person with whom to partner, someone with contacts across a nationwide network with properties and people who could be trusted to operate fairly and effectively.

He had been drawn to a couple from Burkina Faso, invited to the conference to explain the plight of uneducated females, and encourage the delegates to find ways of effective working among polygamous tribal villages.

He was a type A high achiever, and just couldn't wait to get going. Listening to this session wasn't really his thing, but he was enjoying it, fascinated by the speaker who was starting to cut to the quick. There were nervous faces from the hosts and buttocks shifted uncomfortably as he stuck to his courageous message.

'Well I've met a lot of people, some of them are here today, who wouldn't know how to start serving the poor at the expense of their own power, wealth or reputation.

'Let me talk about three precious things. I've found that to mess with any of these three things provokes anger in a human being. These three affect a person more than any other; Money, Moral Authority, Influence.

'Someone steals your money, taxes you higher or cuts your pay and all hell breaks loose; if another comes and rides rough shod all over your influence, brings you down to size or violates your reputation, you're liable to cut up rough; when somebody brings a superior spiritual approach to yours, makes you look weak and ineffectual in your ministry, demonstrates how phony you are, then we'd better all look out for your reaction.

'Jesus wasn't quite like the rest of us. He said, "if you have seen me you have seen the Father." So I guess we'll have to take it that he's given us a pretty good indication of what

makes the Creator angry. Interestingly none of these three things I mentioned made him angry.

'What made him angry was when people treated children wrong, despised or excluded them. He got pretty animated when he found folks working a racket; with the system he'd set up for dealing with guilt. And he was not overly gentle pointing out to those to whom he'd delegated his spiritual authority when he saw them loading up the people with a whole lot of things he'd never asked for.

'I guess I'm saying that he had problems with injustice, selfishness, greed, pride and spiritual abuse.'

Listening transfixed was Benjamin Traoré. He was present at the conference leading a seminar on the importance of grappling with infant malaria. He'd done very well since moving on from Light to Africa, to one of the big boys, United Medical Aid. He had taken on responsibility for their sub–Saharan Africa operation with specific focus on the Sahel Belt. He had made sure that he had responsibility for all budgets, and the appointment of all personnel prior to taking the post and had built quite an empire within the organization. Malaria nets were one of his most profitable enterprises. He sold them to donors for a profit and to beneficiaries for another profit. Life was good.

He had become totally indispensable within UMA knowing that relationships were critical to achieving this end. All the while UMA saw him as their primary contact to government ministers, and vice versa, he was untouchable, allowing him to take quite significant risks. He was an excellent bully, controlling and feared, alone holding passwords to systems and keys to locks. It was impossible for his staff to operate without his personal involvement in many crucial processes. The way he ran things was incredibly inefficient, but it was the only way to protect his power. There were no mechanisms of comment or grievance in his HR system, his people had a straight choice, his way or the highway.

He felt nothing except a growing hatred for this man's words. He wished he could shut them out. They made him feel uneasy, like they came from an authority which he could not control.

The good professor continued resolutely:

'The Kingdom is not a temporary structure, it is a permanent one. All other kingdoms, the kingdoms of this world are temporary, and run by fallen broken human beings like you and me. That's why there is a stark difference between the two categories. In his Kingdom there are no tears, there is no injustice and there are no poor.

'In our kingdoms, of this world, there's lots of poor people. That's a shambles. Poor people don't just happen. They get that way for a variety of reasons. Let me list a few for you:

'They get to be poor because of <u>oppression</u>. Unjust rulers take too much from them, bad neighbours and people with a desire to get more than their share steal from them; markets are rigged against them. The bible lists this kind of poverty in its pages at least 80 times.

'The <u>needy</u> and <u>dependent</u> are the poor who are too old or too young to fend for themselves; orphans and the aged with no families. The bible mentions these 61 times.

'The <u>frail</u>; these people are sick or disabled. They are in need because their body or mind does not work properly. The bible mentions them 57 times.

'The <u>dispossessed</u> are mentioned 31 times. These are your refugees — those who have had their land grabbed over their heads.

'And there's one more cause of poverty that is less external and more volitional. More so than with all the others, this kind of poverty is available to us in the conference room. It is the poverty which comes to us through our own <u>personal poor behaviour</u>.

'Proverbs, in chapter 13 verse 25, tells us that wickedness causes the belly to suffer want. Also, in chapter five verses 10 and 11, too much sleep and want will attack us like an armed robber. Hasty planning is the cause of want in Proverbs 21 five. Proverbs also tells us that oppressing the poor to increase our own wealth, or giving to the rich (see 22:16), or loving pleasure (in 21:17), or miserliness and gambling (in 28:22, for example) — all of these bring us to want. This kind of poverty is caused by personal sin.

'The scriptures also speak of the solution to this, in the opening verse of Psalm 23: "The Lord is my shepherd, I shall not want."'

Joseph and Eve, special guests at the conference were enjoying this. It was their first visit to America, they had come as guests of the organizers, representing women's education needs in Francophone West Africa. They were excited to be in California, the place from where the missionaries had come, back in the 1920s and brought the good news of Jesus with his radical love to their nation.

This man was talking their language.

In the ten years of the existence of Lydia Girls the programme had grown beyond their hopes. Eve was now responsible for a three storey purpose built training facility with an annual intake of 100 girls. The three year programme was nationally recognized for its quality and ingenuity. The range of skills it was able to teach had increased, and its graduates were cropping up all over the country running small businesses, developing employment.

Releasing women into education and vocational development was having a transforming effect on their villages.

The fact that they did not have children of their own was still a matter of personal pain, manageable but constant. Every time they had to deal with an unwanted pregnancy among the girls, Eve in particular had to work hard not to be judgmental. Young women made mistakes, they suffered from coercion, they were raped or tricked. Among 300 young women there was always a percentage who struggled with chastity.

Joseph's work in leading the church had seen over 20 church plants. He was as committed to mission and the development of leaders; and as effective at doing both as his first mentor Michel had been. Of the 20 plus churches he had planted, half had planted on, the most vigourous two or three times already. He avoided high office within the denomination, as supporting Eve with Lydia Girls took a proportion of his time. This together with his commitment to mission and the development of discipleship in and around his villages made his life demanding and totally fulfilling.

There had been some major struggles along the way. He had been defrauded by those smart enough to abuse his trust. He had been taken for granted by foreign missionaries; anxious to do their good deeds to the extremely poor, but unable to see the impact of their mission upon Joseph. He had lost earnings, funded fuel, paid for calls, and incurred heavy food costs without reimbursement. He was however happy to facilitate humanitarian efforts towards his people and remained uncomplaining when a thoughtless philanthropist overstretched his and Eve's meagre resources.

There had been far more encouragements. Friends from Denmark, Sweden and Germany had helped the establishment of chicken farms, pig farms, a water distillation and bottling plant, and dried mango and ground nut production for local and export sales.

Mads and Freja had put their own lives on hold. They had committed themselves utterly to the Lydia Girls. They were no longer part of the smart set in Glostrup. Mads relinquishing leadership of his company and running a small charity instead. This and the downsizing of the house and relying primarily on Freja's income took them down market. Their social death in Denmark had brought community life in Bandaradougou.

Irrigation systems, made locally for good profits and affordably distributed were changing the crop yields. New wells had been dug, and a medical doctor from Ireland had launched a series of clinics, personally raising funds to sustain them, and overseeing the medical staff with regular visits.

There was still no school, though there was a possible partnership with an English academy which had the potential to facilitate one, time would tell.

They didn't have everything they wanted, but they were as sure as they could be that they had come into what God wanted for them so far, and that was good and pleasing.

The speaker continued to nourish their ears.

> *'I want to deal for a moment with money. We claim to be following one who had nothing he called his own and who said, "Sell your possessions and give to those in need. This will store up treasure for you in heaven! And the purses of heaven never get old or develop holes. Your treasure will be safe; no thief can steal it and no moth can destroy it."*

> *'Let us have a little fun for a moment. Take any note paper or tablet you're using, or if you have none imagine you're doing this. On a clean page draw a line down the centre, and to the right side of the paper jot down a list of all the things you have given up or sold in order to give money to people in need. Then on the left side of the paper list your major assets. I'll give you a couple of minutes.'*

He paused to allow the delegates to complete the task. There was a shuffling of papers and a scrabbling for pens across the auditorium.

> *'When you have completed this task, I want you to add a couple of labels to your paper. On the left hand side add the heading "My Bank" and on the right add the heading "Bank of God".*

'Take a look at your paper, and ask yourself the question,

"Which of these banks will be of any use to me 250 years from today?" Then review the state of your accounts.'

There was a wry chuckle around the venue.

'Some of you fall into the trap of one of the perils of joining mission agencies. You can get so drawn into the collective identity that you forget your own. The ends of the mission can become so all important to you that you end up being driven by the needs it meets, and not led by the God who called you to serve there.

'You might even find yourself using a little "evangelastic" when you report on your achievements. Thinking of that it has been a long time since I opened a letter seeking funds that tells a story of failure, of struggle, of apology over the mistaken use of funds. There always seems to be a positive spin on what is happening.

'There are likely some professional consultants who offer to take the story feeds from your field staff, and give them a little spruce up, change a couple of material facts to make the folks with the cheque books write a little bolder. Statistics can have a tendency to get double reported, achievements over–emphasized, failures air brushed out of the story; you know what can happen when you want to look your best.

'Friends hear me on this: that kind of behaviour should not be found in the Kingdom of God. It belongs among the kingdoms of this world where the temporary rulers play their power games, and rip off the masses calling themselves "friends of the people". If that is your practice then it is time to change. You need to stop acting as if the account of Ananias and Sapphira hadn't demonstrated how strongly God feels about it when his people deliberately tell lies about doing good.

'Now I guess you're all doing good stuff. That is business as usual for the Kingdom of God. Do you want to eat and drink with Jesus in his permanent kingdom? Want to participate in lasting leadership for all eternity? Then drop the leadership patterns of the kingdoms of this world. They have no place in the Kingdom of God.'

Rick and Pamela squeezed each other's hands. They knew this was going to come up. Rick was big friends with the speaker, and had sought advice from him in recent months. This part of the talk was rooted in their late night debates over a cold one, wrestling with the issue of the rise of expert fund–raising strategists whose work straddled Christian and non–Christian nonprofits.

Of course there was always pressure on budgets, and big organizations like theirs had complicated and effective action plans to manage the fund–raising process. The challenge had been to keep those systems subservient to the values of the King for whom ultimately they worked — a constant struggle.

Rick had been under pressure over this very issue from his mission agency and had held the line of truth to the point of resigning. He had moved on and was now working for Ablaze church as a teaching pastor, bringing some much needed reforms there from within the leadership team.

He would one day return to his beloved Vietnam, for now his work with Ablaze was a fascinating challenge.

The speaker was reaching the end of his discourse.

'My friends let us learn again to take our place at the back of the line, to prefer others and stop competing with family members for available resource as if the King was not watching our behaviour and assessing our fitness for eternal leadership. Your continued leadership is subject to a law: the survival of the fittest. If you are not fit to lead, your leadership will be taken from you.

'Within the framework set by the values we have discussed, let us take seriously the needs of the poor and address those needs with the resources and the weapons of the Kingdom.

'Let us take the reasons for poverty I mentioned earlier and look at how the King responds and reacts to each:

'Those who are <u>poor because of oppression</u>. We must meet their immediate needs with acts of compassion and generosity; and their long term needs with strategies for giving these people ways of determining their own better future.

'We must also speak the truth to those in power, continually reminding them that they are not unaccountable for their actions. This includes carrying the message of the Creator to despots. Despots can be found ruling over territories, big companies, trafficking systems, crime syndicates, cartels and many other self–serving unfeeling regimes. Carrying an insistence on justice to such people will get some of you killed. Your death will have been worthwhile.

'Those who are <u>needy and dependent</u>. There is a father to the fatherless, a son to the elderly and frail and a husband to the widow. You are his body, continue to be his hands and feet and carry his compassion and care to those who cry to him for help.

'The <u>frail: people sick or disabled</u>. These poor you will always have. Support and initiate beautiful systems for their care. Treat them, love them, include them, share life with them.

'The <u>dispossessed</u> need shelter and as with the oppressed they will need you to carry the voice of truth to those who dispossessed them. This could land you in trouble, see you slandered, violated. Do not back down; those with no voice need yours.

'And finally <u>personal poor behaviour.</u> Never forget that the starting point of becoming a disciple of Christ is the abandonment of rebellion against his values. If you decide

211

you're in, and accept his legal arrangements on your behalf you gain the adopted rights of his own dear children. Do not suppose you can then live out his values without training in righteousness, or receiving his power. For that you will need the third person of God. Be sure to welcome the Holy Spirit, give him an access all areas pass to your life and watch him go to work transforming you.

'Those who oppose you, everyone who runs and supports a system that operates according to values opposed to those owned by the Creator will in due course answer to him for the outcomes of those systems. Tell people what Jesus told people: "Utterly change your behaviour for the Kingdom of God is here."'

Ellen and Garry sat close, legs touching, hands clasped. They were here at the Global Mission Summit as part of Garry's induction programme with Latin Compassion. He had resigned as senior pastor at Ablaze on account of what that role was doing to Ellen. They had spent a little time with Rick and Pamela who had referred them on to a specialist counselor. Garry had been guided back towards his first love; direct mission action among the poor. Pamela felt they had both found release.

'I'll finish with the oft repeated words of the Apostle John, persecuted and exiled for his simple adherence to the principle that if Jesus is Lord, then Caesar is not. He survived his oppressor and saw out his days as an old man in the Turkish city of Ephesus.

'His entreaty I give to you: "Little children love one another, it is the Lord's command and if this alone be done it is enough."'

As the applause died down, Casper headed for the nearest coffee stand. There he encountered a smart intelligent fellow from an outfit called UMA. Casper had visited their exhibition stand the previous day and had been impressed by the delivery credentials of the organization.

Benjamin was anxious to make an impression. He had quickly taken in Casper's TAG Heuer Carrera watch, patent leather shoes and Caraceni suit. Casper was just the kind of person Benjamin liked to meet at these events.

They exchanged brief exploratory greetings and it became apparent to Casper that Benjamin was exceptionally well connected, particularly to government offices in the countries he was most anxious to affect. While not directly involved in food distribution, he may have some contacts that could prove useful.

Their conversation drifted towards the areas where Benjamin had worked in the past, particularly the Burkina Faso Mali border. Here Benjamin was clearly an absolute authority. He knew every imaginable key contact and could talk with great knowledge and confidence of the plight of the villagers in these areas. He had apparently been dispensing free medical services in the region for many years prior to joining UMA.

Casper was amazed and surprised to be talking with a second individual from a very small clearly defined part of Africa within two days. Only yesterday he had enjoyed a fascinating conversation with Pastor Joseph, who had grown up there. Consequently he was able to talk quite knowledgeably with Benjamin, from the detailed information he had gleaned from Joseph. It was almost as if he'd been there himself. He wondered if God might be nudging him in the direction of this area. His interest was certainly kindled.

The remains of their lattes, long finished, slowly turned to congealed sad remnants of foam as their discussion about social justice and the standard of living in the villages lengthened and deepened. Casper began to see in his mind a great synergy possible if he could bring together this highly connected medical doctor, his own significant financial resources and the Pentecostal church network in which Pastor Joseph was an established figure.

His eyes hunted the vestibule of the auditorium for Joseph and Eve, lighting upon them. He caught his breath in excitement, stood quickly, cutting Benjamin off in mid flow as he outlined another strategic contact he would be pleased to introduce.

'Look, there's Pastor Joseph! I think it would be an excellent idea for us to sit down and discuss how the three of us could work together on a programme for stabilizing food prices in his region. Your contacts, his network and a bit of external stimulus could be an incredible combination for transformation. Come and meet him, you and he have a tremendous amount in common.'

Benjamin looked slightly puzzled but such was the obvious potential for huge sums of money to flow through this relationship he allowed himself to be dragged through the crowd to a slightly disheveled young Mossi farmer–pastor and his wife.

'Let's do lunch,' said Casper.

————————————

POSTSCRIPT

The *Education for All* movement was launched at the *World Conference on Education for All* in 1990 by UNESCO, UNDP, UNFPA, UNICEF and the World Bank.

Ten years later, at the World Education Forum on April 26–28, 2000, in Dakar, Senegal, the *Education for All Movement*, representing 164 countries agreed on the *Dakar Framework for Action*.

This is an extract from the agreement:

> *The Dakar Framework*
>
> *Education For All: Meeting Our Collective Commitments*
>
> 7. *We hereby collectively commit ourselves to the attainment of the following goals:*
>
> (i) *expanding and improving comprehensive early childhood care and education, especially for the most vulnerable and disadvantaged children;*
>
> (ii) *ensuring that by 2015 all children, particularly girls, children in difficult circumstances and those belonging to ethnic minorities, have access to and complete, free and compulsory primary education of good quality.*

Over the page there is a photo, taken in February 2013, in which there are eight children. None of them go to school. Four of them have shoes. There are less than two years to the Dakar agreement commitment's deadline.

This book has attempted, among other things, to draw attention to the importance of education, especially for females in polygamous families.

More than anything what is needed is concerted, locally owned, intelligent action for education in communities. This action needs to contend with the inertia and the prevailing conditions which have kept the children of the subject community uneducated.

Those given responsibility for taking action on education developments must have high moral standards and benevolent values in order to deliver against the goal of free compulsory good quality education, without selling out to personal gain.

Local churches when well run, are well placed to take such action. The agape love defined by the life and example of Jesus is selfless and treats the object of its affection as precious to the lover. When a community of people embraces the values of the gospel of Jesus Christ, transforming acts of justice and right actions naturally follow. He commands it, empowers and inspires it.

It may not surprise you to discover that there is a need for a primary school in a situation very similar to the one left unresolved in the fictional Bandaradougou within these pages.

In a little village a few miles from Lafiabougou in the Southern outskirts of the city of Bobo–Dioulasso, stands a grove of eucalyptus trees, planted to prevent anyone building on the plot. This plot has been set aside for a primary school. It is in a village where none of the children go to school. It is served by a nearby church pastor of integrity and with an incredible track record of social justice projects.

There is a project under way to build a school on the plot, in partnership with this pastor. It will be financed by funds raised by a town-wide team based in the UK, working for the charity: Aid to Burkina.

The trees in that little grove are eight years old now and fully grown. A cohort of five year olds has grown up without a primary education whilst the trees have matured. The age and size of the trees is a testimony to a delay which has already cost 400 children (including those pictured) their education, and almost certainly condemned them to a lifetime of poverty.

If you are in a position to help out and would like to do so, then please visit aidtoburkina.org.uk and take it from there.

aidtoburkina.org.uk